COPING WITH CH

COPING
W I T H

Choosing
A College

M.W. Buckalew Jr. and L.M. Hall

ROSEN PUBLISHING GROUP, INC. NEW YORK

Published in 1990 by The Rosen Publishing Group, Inc.
29 East 21st Street, New York, NY 10010

First Edition

Manufactured in the United States of America

Library of Congress Cataloging-In-Publication Data

Buckalew, M. W.
    Coping with choosing a college / M.W. Buckalew
and L.M. Hall—1st ed.
        p.   cm.
    Includes bibliographical references.
    ISBN 0-8239-1079-2
    1. College, Choice of—United States.   I. Hall,
L. M. (Linda Mason)   II. Title.
LB2350.5.B83   1990
378.1'98'0973—dc20
                                        89-28187
                                            CIP
                                            AC

*For
Jennifer
and
Julie*

ABOUT THE AUTHOR ◇

During the writing of this book, Dr. M. Walker Buckalew, Jr., was the President of Cumberland University, located just outside metropolitan Nashville, Tennessee. He is now President of Research for School Management of Wilmington, Delaware, an organization that assists the leaders of private schools around the world with the enhancement of their educational programs.

Dr. Buckalew has also taught at the University of North Carolina at Asheville and St. Lawrence University in Canton, New York, and has been a principal, teacher, and coach in public high schools in North Carolina, West Virginia, and Wyoming. He is a graduate of Duke University and served three years as an officer in the United States Navy.

"This book is a very personal communication from me to young people who are entering their junior or senior years in high school," he writes. "Through long experience I have found that the kinds of problems that really concern them the most—what happens with my friends, how do I decide what I want to do, where can I go to do it—often are not addressed by college publications of various kinds. This book will be different."

Contents

Introduction and Acknowledgments

Bookstore shelves are filled with information about colleges, but the information is only of a certain kind. You can learn about size, location, academic offerings, and expenses in numerous source books. You can find books that may help you perform better on college entrance examinations such as the SAT and the ACT. You can find assistance in getting through the financial aid maze. Most of these volumes are well done. Some examples are *The College Handbook, Peterson's Higher Education Directory, Peterson's Guide to Four-Year Colleges,* and *Guide to College Admissions.*

This book makes no effort to do what those excellent books do so well. This book, instead, is about how to "handle" the whole thing—that is, how to handle your fears, your hopes, your confusions, your excitement, your parents, your friends, your teachers, and the countless other pieces of the college-choosing puzzle that lie closest to the core of you, that core which is facing a completely new stage of your life.

This stage will be different from anything you have experienced before or will experience after. It deserves the special attention that, together, you and I will now give it.

I want to acknowledge the help of four people in particular, although, as you will read, a very large number of college students and their parents helped with the writing of this book by allowing me to interview them.

Mrs. Sally Williams of Brentwood, Tennessee, graciously allowed me to attend a panel discussion that she arranged and conducted in January 1989. The panel comprised nine graduates (now college students) of Brentwood High, a superior public high school on the outskirts of metropolitan Nashville. Mrs. Williams arranged for me to tape the discussion, much of which is reproduced in this book, with the permission of the students.

Ms. Linda Mason Hall, to whom I am married, co-authored the final two chapters of the book. At the university in which she and I administrate and teach, she teaches the required freshman course entitled, "Personal Development." This psychology requirement is a how-to-survive course in which students are taught the basics of succeeding in classes, in the dormitories, in their social lives—and in life beyond the campus. Naturally, she becomes their counselor in this process.

Finally, I want to acknowledge my parents, who more than thirty years ago played just the right role in helping me with my own college-choosing process. They were supportive every day, but they let me make the basic decision. The only thing I was missing was this book!

CHAPTER 1

College: Is It Worth Doing at All?

I am a college president now, but I haven't always been one.

Once I was a sixteen-year-old eleventh-grader. What I thought about college at that point in my life was, frankly, nothing.

I knew that I would graduate from high school the following spring. And what concerned me about the next step in my life was not whether to go to college or not, and it was certainly not what college to attend. What concerned me was my friends. Where would they be? Where would I be? How would we still see each other every day? How would I get along at any college, or in any job, if I could no longer see my friends all the time?

So what I thought about college when I was an eleventh-grader was nothing at all. I didn't want to think about it, and so I did not think about it.

Not all my friends and acquaintances took the same approach that I did. A few of them, I noticed, wrote letters or made phone calls to nearby colleges. They collected brochures and catalogs. They signed up for "college day" visits. They even got information about financial aid and may have, I suppose, discussed all this with their parents and with representatives from a college or two.

Not I. I was determined not to do any of that if I could possibly avoid it. And avoiding it was actually pretty easy.

Psychologists have a name for the way I (and most of my friends) behaved when we were juniors in high school. Our effort simply not to think about the future is termed *denial*. Probably everybody practices denial from time to time. We pretend that problems or potential problems do not exist, and we therefore do not "waste" our time and effort thinking about them.

Psychologists also have a name for the opposite extreme, for worrying about everything that could conceivably happen in the near-term or long-term future. That name is *obsessive behavior*, and it can be at least as damaging and self-destructive as denial.

The healthy way to learn to think and behave falls between the extremes of denial and obsession. It means learning to see the difference between future events that are not worth thinking about and those that really must be thought about if we are to handle them responsibly when they arrive.

It means realizing that losing sleep over the earth's chances of colliding with another planet is self-destructive mental behavior, as is worrying about whether anyone will think you're stupid if you ask questions about going to college. And it means that avoiding the thoughtful consideration of something you know will happen, such as the arrival of your eighteenth birthday and the start of a new phase of your life, is a reasonably sure way to give yourself problems that you otherwise might not have to face at all.

If you are a high school junior now, it is simply time well spent to look thoughtfully at your life two years from today and to begin a process designed to help you arrive at that point a happy, satisfied, even excited person. My purpose in writing this book is to help you feel confident and comfortable with that process. That can be both interesting and fun. So let me see if I can get your attention with the following information.

Several years ago a scientist named Dr. Christopher Jencks formed a team of researchers who studied successful people. He wanted to know what kinds of things seemed to make a difference in whether or not people lived lives that they and others viewed as successful. Here is a summary of Dr. Jencks's findings:

- Finishing high school made little difference in whether or not someone became successful, except in the sense that people usually cannot go to college unless they finish high school.
- The choice of college made almost no difference either.
- Grades earned in college were of little importance.
- Courses of study selected in college made no difference.
- After all the possible factors were studied carefully, only one thing appeared to make a real difference in whether or not a person had a successful life. And that crucial factor was *finishing* college.[1]

We can argue about what success really means, or about what it ought to mean in our society. And we can agree that

[1] Christopher Jencks et al. *Who Gets Ahead? The Determinants of Economic Success in America.* New York: Basic Books, 1979.

success and happiness are not the same thing. But Dr. Jencks's research showed that a college degree opened doors to a great variety of jobs that paid well and commanded respect. It suggested that this would be true for most people, regardless of what college they chose, what their grades were, or what courses of study they pursued.

Is that happiness? Not necessarily. Happiness, as you and I probably found out by the time we were sophomores in high school, mostly has to do with being around a person or people whom you like and who like you.

I want you to acknowledge while you read this book that, once you are no longer a full-time student, you will either have to go to work full time, or be married to someone who is working full time, or both. It is increasingly common in America for both wife and husband to work. It is also increasingly common in America for women who have children to go back to work when the children reach an appropriate age.

If you decide not to go to college, you can certainly still have happiness in your life. But unless you are very unusual, you will be a less successful person than you would have been if you had gone to college and graduated. Why not choose to be happy *and* successful? Why not become determined to have good friendships *and* to find a college you can like?

Think about this. Although it is true, as I feared when I was an eleventh-grader, that after high school graduation things will be very different and you will probably not see your high school friends nearly as frequently, by selecting the "right" college you can greatly increase the chances that you will have more and stronger friendships there than in high school. In other words, people *select* the college they want to attend, whereas in high school people usually are *assigned* to their school. Isn't it more likely that you will find good friends in a place where everyone has made the same choice as you, than in a situation in which you are with others just because they happen to live in the same part of town?

In another well-known research study, Dr. Theodore Newcomb and his team of scientists assigned students at the University of Michigan to live together in certain arrangements and then kept track of their friendships. The students at first reported liking their roommate better than other people. But as time passed the students reported liking those students with whom they had the most in common. They preferred students whose attitudes and values were like their own over the students who happened to be assigned to them as roommates.[2]

If you decide that going to a college is the right thing for you to do, and if you follow the suggestions I shall make as to how to make that choice, you will greatly increase your chances of placing yourself in a college where large numbers of your classmates share your own attitudes and values. If you choose your college in this way, then, you not only increase your odds of being successful in your career but also of being happy while you are there.

My son's first choice of college was a terrible one. Not only did he not begin to think about it when he was a high school junior, he did not even think about college seriously until after he had graduated! In midsummer that year he and I hastily found a convenient school that would take him at that late date, which may have been worse than not doing anything at all. As you might imagine, his freshman year was pretty miserable. He had left a high school class

[2] T.M. Newcomb. *The Acquaintance Process*. New York: Holt, Rinehart & Winston, 1961.

full of good friends in exchange for a school in which he was unlikely to find many people like himself.

As a result, he was unhappy. And he was not very successful as a student. Often, as you know, those two things go together. An unhappy person does not very often succeed. That is why I am urging you to think now about the college choice-point in your life. If you do it right, you can find yourself surrounded by many good friends, you can be taught by teachers who at least in some ways share your own attitudes and values, and you can eventually graduate and move into a career that you will like and in which you will find success.

My son asked me at the end of that first year if I thought he should drop out of college. I told him that I thought he needed to do then what I am asking you to do now: to think carefully about himself, his future, and what he hoped to find during at least the following ten years or so of his lifetime.

He dropped out and moved to Chicago, hundreds of miles from family or friends except for one who lived in that city. Since he had learned to type well in high school, he was able to get a job with a good company, and within a year or so he had been promoted several times. And then a funny thing began happening. His bosses began telling him that he ought to quit his job! Their point was really the same one made by Dr. Jencks's research team. My son had already advanced as far as he could in that company without a college degree. It did not matter that he was smart and capable. He simply could go no further without his college diploma. And, as Dr. Jencks found, it did not really matter what the college might be, or even what he might study there. He simply needed to go back to college and, this time, finish the job.

So on this second try he chose carefully. He obtained

material. He made phone calls. He went to see for himself. He talked to people. Above all, he understood why he was making the choice. He was looking for both happiness— that is, people who seemed to be like him—and success— that is, a college that fit him well enough so that he could happily finish its course of study.

It worked. He found friends. He graduated. He has an exciting job and many choices as to what to do with his life. Furthermore, he found the young woman with whom he may spend the rest of his life. That remains to be seen, but you do see my point. By placing himself in an environment that fitted him, he found both happiness and success. He found people to like and love and who would like and love him. And he found a situation in which he could succeed, and which would lead to further success.

What about his father? I must admit that my life and career have turned out all right, despite my unwillingness as an eleventh-grader to do anything but deny that my college choice-point had arrived. Frankly, I was lucky.

In the fall of my senior year my parents obtained some college admissions materials from four schools. (In Chapter 2, "Who Decides?", I will discuss the role your parents might or might not play in all this.) Still I did not study the material or give the situation any thought. I continued to practice psychological denial.

Eventually, however, I did fill out the forms for the four colleges. And when three of my friends invited me to go with them to visit one of the colleges, I agreed to go, if for no other reason than that it sounded like an interesting day.

Although I enjoyed the trip, the visit itself was a disaster. Since I was completely unprepared, I had no plan of action. I had nothing to ask the Admissions Counselor who spoke to me at the Admissions Office. I made no effort to talk to any of the students. I did not even have lunch in the dining hall. (If you live on a college campus, you will probably eat more than a thousand meals in the dining hall by the time you graduate; doesn't it make sense to give the food a try during your visit?)

I even encountered one of those situations that you always remember as "life's most embarrassing moments." One of my friends was almost as poorly prepared as I was. As a result, he and I were finished at the Admissions Office long before our better prepared friends. We wandered over to an adjacent building, which turned out to be the library. At nearly all colleges the library is a separate building, whereas in most high schools it is merely a room in the main classroom building.

We strolled into the first room we found. Much later I was to learn that this was the reference room, where dictionaries, encyclopedias, and other basic assistance volumes were kept. The room was no bigger than our high school's library and had about the same number of books. Something told me, though, that this library had thousands—maybe even hundreds of thousands or millions—of books housed elsewhere in the building.

That thought did not, however, occur to my friend. He leaned cockily against the librarian's desk, looked around the room at the books and at the several dozen students who were studying, and said in a tone of voice that could be heard all over the room, "Is *this* all the books you got here?"

Humiliated, I crept out of the reference room. And although the college visit was terrible simply because I was so totally unprepared, I somehow was accepted to that school. I do remember being pleased to receive the acceptance letter several months later. Since some of my friends had chosen that school, and since my girlfriend had decided to attend a college only twenty-five miles away, I informed the school, my friends, and my parents that this would be my college.

I roomed during my first year with a friend from high school and during my second year with another friend from high school. Since I had those two and several other friends, and since my girlfriend was nearby (although that didn't last), and since—mostly by luck—I was able to find courses that were appealing to me, I became quite happy there and reasonably successful. I certainly had done nothing to deserve either. Circumstances just happened to fall into place for me.

I urge you to do better than I did and better than my son did, too. I was lucky enough to find happiness and success on the first try, despite lack of preparation. My son was not so lucky, nor are many young people who do not make thoughtful preparation. Denial, as I have said, is a very high-risk way to run your life.

THE REV. WILLIAM VESTAL

The Rev. Vestal's college story should be of great interest to you. He is now a psychotherapist and a minister. But once he was a high school student faced with an uncertain future.

Bill Vestal loved high school. He was very popular and very successful. He had many friends, participated in a wide range of activities, was elected to various offices, was a successful athlete, was looked upon as a leader, and had excellent grades.

Understandably, what Bill wanted from college was exactly what he had in high school: good friends, good grades, broad experience, acclaim, and success.

When Bill selected a college, he had thought carefully about the chances of finding his high school experience again. But he had *not* thought through the probabilities. If you are a leader in a school with several hundred students in your class, what are the probabilities of your being equally a leader in a college with more than a thousand students in its freshman class (or, in some cases, many thousands of students)? If you are one of the top students in your high school class, what are the probabilities that you will also be a top student in your college freshman class, which will be larger and perhaps better academically?

If your friends were important to you in high school, what are the probabilities that you will have numerous good friends immediately at a college that is hundreds of miles from home, in another part of the country, and in a setting where there is no particular likelihood that the students will share your attitudes and values?

As I said, Bill Vestal had not thought through the probabilities. He simply applied to what he knew was a "very good school." It happened to be the college at which I found myself, although my own reasons for being there were in no way like Bill's I was there "just because" several friends were. Bill had come a long, long way to this college because he wanted to lead, to be acclaimed, to be popular, and to make top grades at this "very good school."

He and I knew each other very little during those four years. I knew his name; he knew mine. As far as he and I can remember, we never actually did anything together, and perhaps never had a single conversation.

Not long ago, with a group of classmates, I was putting together the program for my twenty-fifth class reunion. In addition to the usual reunion "stuff," I wanted to have at least one serious event when we now middle-aged graduates might get together for an hour or two to think about the preceding twenty-five years plus the four years of college that had brought us together in the first place, nearly thirty years earlier.

We decided to have a panel discussion featuring four of our classmates, who would talk for about five minutes each about how their college experience looked now that a quarter-century had passed. We wanted the audience to join the discussion afterward, so we needed panelists who would tell interesting stories about themselves that might stimulate others to join the discussion.

We looked through the information we had at hand about ourselves and our classmates, and we selected four likely ones. Bill Vestal was one. He was both a psycho-therapist and a minister, and his family and career histories seemed of possible interest to our imagined audience.

When I phoned Bill, whom I had not seen since college graduation, it was as if we had been best friends for years. It was as if we had last spoken with each other the day before. Incredible as it may seem, he had only weeks before my call composed a letter to his classmates of twenty-five years before.

He wanted us to learn from his experience, and so he was writing to us. When I asked him to be on our panel, he decided just to bring his letter and read it to us in person. And so he did.

As you read Bill Vestal's letter, I want you to think about the title of this chapter: "College: Is It Worth Doing at All?" I want you to think about that question and to think about the kinds of things Bill Vestal *could* have done as a high school student in order to have saved himself from what happened to him in college—and after college.

I must tell you, too, that Bill cried at times while he read this letter to the audience at our twenty-fifth reunion. And I must tell you that many in the audience were crying

harder than he was, because they had experienced the
same devastating things he described:

Dear Classmates, Class of 1962:
    I have just finished filling out the Reunion Ques-
tionnaire. It is the middle of the night, and I want to
"let go" of something I have been coming to terms
with since our time together in college. You will probably never even know I've shared these thoughts/
this journey with you; nevertheless. . .
    I loved our college and my time there, and what the
school and my education stood for then and has come
to stand for now. I would choose it again, and would
hope a child of mine might as well. However—in the
midst of all that positive experience and memory and
feeling—something in me never quite "clicked." Our
college blew "me" away—I lost my "self" (or perhaps
found that I simply never knew/had my "self" to lose)!
So, despite all the "good," what I wrestled with most
for the first twenty years after graduation was the
PAIN—the scars, the confusion, the emptiness, the
opening of a wound I *brought* there (yet had no notion
really of its depth) and my real failure to close and heal
it before I left you.
    Oh, I knew a few of you and a few of you knew me;
I touched many of you and many of you touched me.
Yet, through it all, I NEVER REALLY QUITE GOT
HOLD OF "ME"—OF A PERSON I WAS, BUT
THOUGHT I HAD TO QUALIFY OR SELL OR
PROVE. So I never quite "took hold" of you or the
classwork or the experience. I came to you at seventeen convinced that I was a guy who could handle most
anything well and belonged "up front—leading and
shaping." And though I shared that energy and con-

fidence and risking with you (on the *outside*) over those four years, *inside* something else was happening. MY "IDENTITY" WAS COLLAPSING!!! I wasn't leading or shaping in any way that I deemed significant (academically, socially, politically, athletically); most of the pieces of "ME" that I valued coming into college didn't seem "good enough"; I wasn't "special," and I didn't have a solid enough "ME" down inside to handle that and affirm my self and grow up.

So I retreated to what seemed to work for me coming in, and (in essence) stayed seventeen for the next twenty years! Oh, I *looked* good—but, in the end, *inside*, I wasn't making it (frequent job changes, constantly overextended, lots of initiative with little follow-through; the marriage failed, the parenting was erratic, the ministry confused, the teaching rebellious, the relationships hurtful). I had recurring nightmares of college (terrifying exams, not finding a new room in the dorms, being lost in a sea of insignificance, crying and alone). As I worked intensely in psychotherapy for fifteen of those twenty years, I sought to unite/reunite the two parts of "ME" and finally to grow up.

For what our college and you (my classmates) had done for me (like the Enchanter to Don Quixote in "La Mancha") was to *hold up the mirror of a reality I had never faced*—a "ME" I had chosen not to know or deal with, the "ME" that was battered and hurting and needy and insecure and terrified and not number one (or anywhere close) and had little idea of where to turn for affirmation. (Thank God for the Methodist Student Center—I actually don't think I would have made it emotionally without the "home/recognition" I found in those walls and activities and people and that Spirit.)

I came back for our twentieth reunion. I saw some of you and talked to a few of you. But mostly I walked ...and remembered...and walked...and wept and hurt and even smiled...and walked...and began to heal! I began to let go of the demons, the demands, the expectations, the almosts, and the failures. I began to simply walk with *me*, and love *me*, and accept *me*—to grieve a "death" of long ago and release it.

Who was I then? Where have I been and who am I now? What has surprised me most and/or turned out differently than I expected? What about my hopes and expectations, successes and disappointments? I guess I'm really summarizing much of that here. I am still amazed at how long it has taken me to "face the mirror" of my college experience, the depth of the journey, and the incredible PAIN I have known. I wonder if others of you have walked this way, too? If you, too, have faced such a mirror that, when you shifted or the light shifted, actually became a window?

I have grown and healed much these past twenty-five years and am coming to know a "peace" I had never imagined—a calmness, a "letting." I guess I'm finally "growing up," and coming to terms with the "ME" who is me—and I am enjoying the process and me, finally. It will be good to see some of you again, and many of you for (perhaps) the first time.

Peace and Joy,
Bill

And we, Bill Vestal's classmates, found it indeed good to see him again, and, for many of us, to see this sensitive, accomplished person from our past for the first time.

For much of the nearly thirty years, then, between Bill

Vestal's high-school graduation and his twenty-fifth college reunion, he was not the happy and successful person he had been in high school and now has again become. *Your own life does not need to follow this pattern*, a pattern that is certainly much more common than it should be. The college I had attended, and every other college across America, had been filled with bright, capable young people who had never really been taught how to make the choice.

KAREN OLDHAM

Karen is currently a senior at the university of which I am President. She has had an exciting, rewarding, fulfilling college career. She is, in fact, now serving her second term as president of the student body. Her leadership has surpassed that of any other student leader I have ever known.

How was she different in high school from my son, or from me? Here are her own words, spoken near the end of the Fall semester of her final year in college:

When I was a junior in high school I began to get admissions materials.... I had taken the ACT, which was the prerequisite for getting into colleges, and I was pretty nervous about that because I wanted to score well on it.... That kind of passed by, and it was probably the last time that I really, really thought about college until late in my junior year.

I just didn't think too much about going to school at that time. I felt that I wanted to go, but I was so involved in clubs and cheerleading that I just didn't want to devote time to thinking about choosing a college. I felt that I had a lot of time yet. Sometimes college seemed so distant in my future that I thought I might die or something before I even got there or actually completed it.

But by the time I was a senior in high school, choosing a college became very, very important to me. I wanted to make the right decision. . . . My family is very close-knit, and because of that each member of my immediate family (my mother, my father, and my sister) was integral in helping me make the decision. . . .

Looking back, I realize that I didn't study the options as much as I should have. Some of the facts that I should have paid attention to, I really didn't think about, like the size of the school, or the friendliness and concern of the teachers, or the exact academic and other programs. More than anything else, I was concerned about how I would finance my education.

Even Karen, happy and successful as she has been in her college years, was not taught to think carefully through the college choice-point in her life. And yet it is obvious that even in high school she was wiser and more thoughtful than many of us. As the second-ranking student in her class, she was asked, along with the class valedictorian, to make a speech at graduation. Here is her recollection of that occasion:

On the night of my graduation I told the audience that we must be able to accept change because change is a certainty. As I saw it, life is like a series of doorways. These doorways represent important stages in our lives like birth, going to school for the first time, graduating from high school, entering college, marriage, accepting your first real job, the birth of your first child, retirement, and death.

As we walk through these doors, the one behind us shuts and locks, but the one in front of us opens to new things. Although the doors we have passed through can never be opened again, we will always have the memories of yesterday to hold on to, and we will have experiences that we can use in walking through the continuous series of doors. Entering new doors, new stages of our lives, creates a certain amount of fear of the unknown in each of us. I think that is probably the single most important fear that a high school student encounters, because he or she knows that college is going to be different but doesn't know how to lessen that fear.

Fear. It raises its ugly head every day of our lives, each time we begin something new and unfamiliar. To an extent, every single day has something unknown or unpredictable lying in wait for us, but that is especially true when, as Karen said, we open a new door to a new stage of our lives and realize that the door to what had become so familiar has closed and locked behind us forever.

You will remember Karen said that her main concern in thinking about college was how she would pay for it. On the evening of her high school graduation, the university notified her that she had been granted a full four-year scholarship. That settled the matter for her, and she enrolled at this school four years ago because it was fully paid for.

You can see, then, that despite Karen's young wisdom and her eagerness to go to the "right" school, her college choice was only a little more thoughtful and planned than Bill Vestal's choice, or my son's, or my own. But Karen, like me, was lucky in her choice. Here are some of her comments about how things turned out for her:

As for friendships in high school compared to the ones I have had in college, there is no comparison. In high school my time was so filled with clubs and other activities, and classes themselves took up so much of each day, that I didn't make a lot of close friends. But at college that changed tremendously.

Suddenly I had friends from all walks of life. I had rich friends, poor friends, extremely intelligent friends, not so intelligent friends, devoutly religious friends, and atheist friends. The diversity was so much greater than it had been in high school. Yet most of the students at my college have a common background. We are mostly from small towns in this part of the state.

Karen, in other words, happened to be offered a scholarship at a school where, despite the diversity she talks about, most of the students had backgrounds just like hers. They were from small towns (and usually from small high schools) in a particular part of this state. Even though many of them were "different," a basic similarity of background ran through the whole student body. As a result, both the quality and the number of her close friendships expanded hugely.

Ask yourself this. If you found yourself at a college with that many wonderful and close friendships, would it not be very hard not to be happy? And if you were that happy, don't you think your chances of succeeding would be very good?

And this, too. Do you not suspect that there are ways to find that kind of "just right" college situation for yourself *on purpose*, rather than by chance?

Before we leave Karen, I want you to hear a little more from her. In discussing her friendships in college, she makes another important point. She notes that in most college situations the students who have chosen to be serious about college are easier to get along with:

> We have all matured a little bit. In high school kids are so immature that they can be cruel a lot of times. But all that changed from the very first day at college. ...I've got the closest friends I have ever had, and they have become a very important part of my life.

We will hear a little more from Karen Oldham in Chapter 6, "The First Year: How Will It Be?" For now, though, it is enough to learn from her how "perfect" going to college can be if you find just the right "fit."

IS IT WORTH DOING?

Asking the question that way suggests a trade-off. When we ask ourselves whether something is "worth it," we mean that we are wrestling with the question of whether the effort and agony and misery of working at something is worth the result that we can expect when it is over. Since Karen has made it clear that there need not necessarily be agony and misery—although certainly there will be effort —attached to attending and graduating from college, I need to rephrase the question: "What do I do now to give myself an excellent chance to be happy in college and to graduate?"

We have discussed the fact that *graduation* from college is the key factor in a successful life, according to Dr. Jencks's research. We have also discussed the importance of happiness and close friendships in setting an environment in which you can expect to succeed.

To enhance your chances for a happy, successful college

experience and graduation, consider taking action immediately, as follows:

- Assess yourself, your interests, and your needs as early in your high school career as you can.
- Involve either your parents or other adults you trust (or both) in the process right away.
- Get *first-hand* information about any college you are seriously considering.
- Above all, remember that your objective is to fit yourself to a school in order to have the most supportive environment possible and thereby ensure your ultimate success: graduation.

I shall discuss the first item, assessing yourself, in just a moment.

I shall discuss the second item, involving your parents or other adults you trust (or both), in Chapter 2, "Who Decides?"

I shall discuss the third item, getting first-hand information about any college you are seriously considering, in Chapter 3, "How Can I Be Certain?"

As for the fourth item, getting the perfect fit in order to have the most supportive environment possible to ensure your ultimate success, that has been the theme of this chapter and will remain the theme throughout the rest of the book. It is the major idea of which I absolutely must convince you.

ASSESSING YOURSELF

Table I is a series of questions that you can ask yourself now. They will assist you in getting a feel for your preferences, especially those that would have a bearing

Table I Thinking About College: A Self-Assessment

Rate yourself on each of the following items. To do this carefully, number one through fifteen on a sheet of paper (which you may want to keep, to see if you change as the months go by). Give yourself a "10" for each item for which you would give the strongest possible *Yes*. Give yourself a "1" for each item for which you would give the strongest possible *No*. Give yourself numbers in between to show various degrees of agreement or disagreement.

Any number from one to ten can be used as an answer to any of these items. You will not be adding the numbers together when you finish.

	Rating (1–10)
1. Grades are extremely important to me.	____
2. It is important to me that all my teachers know my name.	____
3. It is important to me that all my teachers enjoy teaching.	____
4. It is important to me that all my teachers have great reputations as researchers.	____
5. It is important to me that many of the students in my classes be "like me" (have similar values, beliefs, likes and dislikes, etc.).	____
6. It is important to me that I personally know the administrators at my school.	____
7. It is important to me that I personally know some of the students who play on my school's athletic teams.	____
8. I like to attend entertainment events (performances) frequently, such as concerts, movies, and other shows.	____
9. I like to be able to attend large parties.	____
10. I like being with a small group of friends.	____
11. I like being with just one close friend at a time.	____
12. It is important to me to have friends who think the way I do.	____
13. It is important to me to have friends of my religious faith.	____
14. It is important to me to have friends who like to talk about the problems we share.	____
15. I enjoy being by myself.	____

upon your choice of college. In Chapter 5, "What Kind of College? Which One? What About My Friends?" I shall discuss your academic goals and objectives, if you have already developed them. For now, let's continue to look only at your personal preferences.

I suggest that you get a piece of paper and pen and actually write your answers to the fifteen questions, not just once, but twice. Most of you will give slightly different answers to the questions if you answer them the first time for your current (high school) situation and a second time for how you *expect* to feel once you reach college.

When you have answered the questions, circle each 1, 2, 9, and 10. These represent your strongest preferences. If you did the assessment twice, you can see whether or not you expect your preferences to stay the same or to change when you enroll in college.

Having thought carefully about your strongest preferences, you are in a good position to continue with the other steps needed to make sure that your college decision is the precisely right one for you. Fold your answer paper into the book at Table I; I will refer back to these questions and your answers throughout the book. Keep your answers in mind as you read Chapter 2, "Who Decides?" and Chapter 3, "How Can I Be Certain?" By the time you reach Chapter 4 on stress management you should have clear ideas about your preferences, the involvement of your parents or other trusted adults, and the process of getting first-hand information about any college you may seriously consider. All of this, remember, has the sole purpose of making sure that your choice is as perfect as it can be—the perfect fit.

CHAPTER 2

Who Decides?

s we begin to consider the question of who really makes the decision about college, you should have four important points clearly in mind:

1. This chapter has as its theme the second of the recommendations I made in Chapter 1: Involve either your parents or other adults you trust (or both) in the process right away.

2. This chapter assumes that you worked through the fifteen items in Table I. Any discussion you have with any adult about going to college should include those items and your responses to them. Do you see what I am getting at? *You must have help from at least one adult you trust, but you must be absolutely certain that your strong personal preferences form the basis for any such discussion.* Otherwise, even the best-intentioned adult will unwittingly help you select the college at which he or she, rather than you, would fit perfectly.

3. Despite my emphasis in Chapter 1 on the importance of graduation from college for your lifelong

chances for success and happiness, I want to stress here a closely related point. Most four-year colleges, most two-year junior colleges, and even some very good community colleges and technical colleges have as a major goal providing you with a liberal arts education, no matter what field of study you choose to emphasize. I will explain this in more detail in Chapter 5, but for now just bear in mind that most colleges will be preparing you for success and happiness partly by making you an "educated woman" or an "educated man." If they succeed, you will be more interested in reading history, or novels, or the editorial pages of the newspaper than you would otherwise have been. In other words, you will be forever interested in continuing to learn. And those interests, in turn, will underlie the success you can expect to find and the happiness you can hope to experience.

4. Finally, bear in mind this very encouraging fact: Colleges now want you—no, it's more than that— colleges now actually *need* you more than they ever have in history. If you were to stop reading right this second and write notes to five colleges asking for a copy of their catalog, I can assure you that five catalogs would quickly turn up in your mailbox. More amazing still, you would probably receive from several of the five either a letter or a phone call from an Admissions Counselor, asking if she or he might assist you in any way. Believe it or not, you are exactly what many colleges are looking for. No matter what you are like or how much you have accomplished or not accomplished in high school, Admissions Counselors are being paid solely to find you, talk to you, and persuade you

that their college is your perfect fit. You and the trusted adult you have selected, thinking about your answers in Table I, can decide for yourselves whether or not a particular Admissions Counselor is right about that. The point is that there are colleges that will pursue you as soon as you tell them you are interested. In these times of great competition among colleges for high school graduates, you are much more likely to have to talk yourself out of several college invitations than to have to talk yourself into one.

Those are the points you need to remember as we approach the issue of "Who Decides?" Since I suspect that you may not be convinced of that fourth point, here is an example.

The college of which I am President, like every good college in America by now, has carefully defined its "mission." Our mission is to provide a certain kind of education "primarily to rural populations raised on those same educational principles." What does that mean? It means that we have geared ourselves mainly to serve young people who graduate from the small farming communities in this region. Most of those communities have small high schools.

Even though our college is small, many of the high school juniors and seniors who visit our campus comment on what a "big place" it seems to be. We know that we can be a good home to these students. And we, like every other good college in this country, now work very hard to go to all those little high schools, find those students who are interested in college and who can succeed in our courses of study, and bring them to our campus. We know from experience the kind of student most likely to be happy and successful here, and we work very hard to recruit all such students.

But so does every other college. You will, then, have a great deal of help—maybe more than you would like at times—from colleges that think you might be interested in getting your education there.

Having covered these introductory points and, I hope, having convinced you of the fourth, it is time to think about who that "trusted adult or adults" should be. Maybe you already know. Maybe not. Either way, let's talk briefly about what you are really looking for in that person.

First, realize that the person does not have to "qualify" for the role of being your helper. He or she does not necessarily have to be a college graduate, nor someone who is related to you, nor a professional helper of some sort. You need to have at least one adult closely involved with you not because you require a certain *kind* of assistance, but because you need to hear a more experienced voice, the voice of someone who has lived long enough to have experienced "life beyond the teen years."

You have heard the old joke about the teenager who thought his dad was the dumbest person he had ever talked to until he grew up and began to see for himself what adults call "the real world." He decided then that much of what his dad had been saying for years was pretty wise, and he finally acknowledged it in a roundabout way by saying, "Dad seems to be getting smarter as he gets older."

Life does teach some lessons. You need to be in regular contact during your college decision time with at least one adult whose only advantage over you is that she or he has lived longer. Even if you reject every single idea or suggestion that this trusted adult advances, I want you to have the benefit of hearing what that person says. If you remain "true" to your own strong preferences as reflected in your responses in Table I, you will get the college that does fit you. But you will be more certain to make that judgment well if you are challenged by an older mind. Give yourself the chance to consider your decision through the eyes of someone well beyond the teen years. The chances are good that you will not be sorry.

Let me illustrate what I mean. Ten years ago, when I was a professor at another university, a woman came to me for help with a very stressful situation.

Her son had come home from his sophomore year in college and announced to her and his father that he wanted to return to the same college that fall, but with three changes: (1) he wanted to move out of the dormitories and into an off-campus apartment; (2) he wanted to get a part-time job; and (3) he wanted to become a part-time, rather than a full-time, student. His mother was horrified. She found it impossible to agree with him that he would be happier and more successful under those circumstances.

Her husband, on the other hand, thought it was a fine idea. To him, it seemed that his son was just advancing one more step into adulthood by moving out of the college neighborhood and by going to work part time. The mother looked at it as a step toward dropping out of college and was extremely stressed by the thought that her son would never graduate.

The son knew that the answer to the question, "Who Decides?" is: "The student does." But he also knew that listening to adults' expressions of support or opposition is "good business." He knew that experience is a good teacher, and that asking adults who cared about him for their opinions about his decisions was an important part of being sure of the decision—or, possibly, of considering altering the decision in some way.

If he could have reached into the future, found the book

you are reading right now, filled in his responses to Table I, and then discussed them with his mother, he would have had an easier time with her. He and she could have looked thoughtfully at his strong personal preferences rather than becoming opponents immediately. If she had known his personal preferences and had known that he had actually thought carefully about each one, she would have had much less trouble understanding his decision.

What you can learn from that family's crisis is that the trusted adult or adults you select can be your teammates in considering your college choice, no matter how strongly you and they may differ on your assumptions about college. If you start with your own strong preferences, show them that you have already worked through those items, and ask for their comments before you announce your final decision, your objectives can probably be met nicely. And what are those objectives? If you are like most of us, I think they could be listed as follows:

1. You want the adult or adults to know that you do have strong personal preferences.
2. You want the adult or adults to know that you want mainly to hear their thoughts about how your preferences might be made to fit perfectly with a particular college or colleges or type of college.
3. You want the adult to feel "consulted with," rather than "attacked," and you expect the same courtesy in return.

If you accept those objectives and make them clear to your trusted adult, you have an excellent chance of being helped to weigh your decision by an adult who respects and admires you for the careful way you are going about it, who understands what you are hoping to accomplish, and who becomes just what you need: a more experienced mind, thinking hard about how *your* preferences can be turned into the college experience that "fits."

This adult you select—a parent, a teacher, a coach, a counselor, your principal, your minister or priest or rabbi, a neighbor, an uncle or aunt, an older brother or sister, your supervisor at your after-school or summer job—can be any older person you trust to listen to your strong preferences. But be aware that you need for this adult to do more for you than that, as important as that will be.

You will want this person to help you write a good note to college Admissions Offices, to talk with you about interviewing and about the "interview day," to help you fill out financial aid forms, to look with you at college catalogs, and maybe to help you with transportation when you are ready to visit several campuses. I shall talk in detail about each of those and more in Chapter 3 and other chapters, but reading this book and talking these things over with a trusted adult are two different things, both of which are needed steps in getting the right college fit.

You have already figured out that the ideal arrangement is for you to have several adults who would like to be involved, and for each of them to read this book along with you. That way, each involved person is reading the same material, thinking over the suggestions, and then talking with each other and with you with the same information in hand.

Maybe you can arrange for this ideal set of circumstances, and maybe not. Think, though, about how you can come as close to it as possible. The closer you can come, the better your chances to get the college situation most likely to bring you happiness and success.

Who is the person most likely to be either your one trusted adult or, at least, one of your several trusted adults? My own experience with young people indicates that it is your mother. Here are several examples.

SHELONDA MANNING

Shelonda is a sophomore in college and at the end of her freshman year was elected Secretary of the Student Council. Since her school elects its student council officers in a general election in which the entire student body votes, she is also the Secretary of the student body.

As a black high school student in a predominantly white area, Shelonda gave serious thought to selecting a predominantly black college. She wondered how it might be to study in a situation in which she would no longer be a "minority student."

In the end, though, she chose a predominantly white college, and she has obviously been successful there. What led her to decide against attending a predominantly black institution?

Shelonda's answer is clear: her mother!

> I really wanted to go to the predominantly black state university, which is about an hour's drive from my home. I knew it would be less expensive than a private college, and I wanted to see how it would be to be in the majority for once.
>
> My mother didn't care very much about the racial mixture of my college, though. She just wanted me to be as close to home as possible. We knew that the closest college was this predominantly white school, which is just about twenty miles from home.
>
> I told her that being closer to home would be good, and that I didn't mind continuing to be a minority,

since that was the way it was in high school, and I liked my high school. But, I asked her, how can we afford a private college?

She told me there would be financial aid, and that we would just figure it out. So we did.

LESLIE REECE

Leslie is also a sophomore in college. Like Shelonda, she is active on the Student Council. She has a full-time job as an assistant manager at a fast-food restaurant. Her mother, like Shelonda's, played the lead role as her trusted adult. Leslie recalls it this way.

During my senior year in high school I began thinking, "Well, maybe I don't really want to go to college. I've been working and going to school for a long time, and maybe I just want to take it easy for a while." Gradually, though, I changed my mind and decided to go.

My mother was from the area we had moved to for my last years in high school, and she really wanted me to try the local college. It was small, and I thought I would probably be comfortable there, so I decided to try it.

My guidance counselor in high school didn't like the idea. She said, "You really could get into a better school, Leslie." And I thought, "Well, what does 'better' mean? Does it mean bigger? Does it mean a school with more academic programs and majors and more prestige? What could be better for me than a small school near my home?"

I admit that my mother's wishes really influenced

me, but I also felt eventually that she was right. Finally, I did apply, and I was given a good scholarship; that helped me to decide.

So I thought, I'll go to this small school for two years, and then I'll transfer to a bigger one.

Well, now that I'm finishing my sophomore year I've decided that I don't really want to transfer. I've decided to stay and graduate from this school.

I can say that I've chosen the right school for me, with my mother's help. This college is not for everybody, but no school is for everybody. Here I've made so many friends and gotten involved in everything, and I've liked the academic part, too. So I've been very happy with my—and her—choice.

MRS. MARTHA BRADSHAW

Shelonda and Leslie say that their mothers were greatly influential in their college choice, and so do many other college students. Let's hear what one particular mother has to say about this. Unlike Shelonda's and Leslie's mothers, Mrs. Martha Bradshaw had a large, prestigious college in mind for her oldest son.

I was deeply involved in my oldest son's choice of college. We began early in his junior year in high school with the ACT and SAT tests. We knew that his scores on those would determine just how selective a college we could hope for him to attend.

He scored very well on both, and that put him in line to choose a selective school. We then began the visitation process. We visited schools all over our region.

Because he was our first child, we probably went

overboard on the college admissions process and applied to far more schools than was really necessary. I believe we formally applied to seven schools.

He was accepted to all of them. He also received a Naval Reserve Officers Training Corps (NROTC) scholarship that he could use at the school of his choice, provided, of course, that the school had an NROTC program. That helped make the decision easier.

During all of that two-year process [junior and senior high school years], we spent quite a bit of time on the applications. He was so busy that I helped him with the applications in many ways. I helped in writing for material, typing the application essays that he had written by hand, getting them copied and ready for mailing, and so on.

I also worked hard at helping him secure his scholarship in that he didn't have time to do all the busywork needed. I did whatever I could to help.

WHO DECIDES?

I think several things are obvious. First, adult involvement can be important in making the right choice. Second, the decision is basically your own. Third, there is no single "correct way" to go through the process. It is true that I recommend strongly that you begin with Table I, but even that step you should take only if you agree that it is a good starting point. If you do start there, you can involve adults with less risk that the college decision will become theirs rather than your own.

BRENTWOOD HIGH SCHOOL
PANEL DISCUSSION

This top-ranking school is in Brentwood, Tennessee, a small city near Nashville. Brentwood High annually sends about nine out of every ten graduates to college. The college choice-point is so significant to nearly all the school's juniors and seniors that the parents and counselors hold a panel discussion in midyear during which recent graduates discuss college choices and college life.

I refer frequently in this book to the January 1989 session at Brentwood High. For now, let me report on just a few of the interesting facts and opinions expressed by the graduates, now college freshmen or sophomores.

Asked whether any particular adult or adults were importantly involved in their college decision process, about half of the panelists said, "No, I did it all myself." The others, males and females, said that their mothers were heavily involved in the choosing. One mentioned that, in addition to his mother, an Admissions Counselor at the college he eventually chose was helpful and influential.

Did they all choose well? No. Some were clearly very happy and successful, whereas others were less so. Two of the students, both of whom are quoted later, began at large universities and transferred to small ones.

Did any students find happiness and success in college without involving any adult at all in the choosing process? Certainly. Does that mean you should try it, too? Not at all. Involvement of a trusted adult can only help you provided you work through Table I before you begin and then insist that your own strong preferences be honored.

Table II is designed to help you sort through the adults in your life who might play this vital role in your choosing. As with Table I, there is no final score. Both tables are

Table II Thinking About Adults: Who Are the Possibilities?

To do this carefully, number 1 through 17 on a sheet of paper (which you may want to keep, to see if you change as the months go by).

Rate each of the following adults on a scale of 1 to 10, depending upon how good a listener she or he seems to be, how friendly she or he usually is, and how available she or he could probably be. Assign a 10 if the person is an excellent listener; another 10 if extremely friendly; and another 10 if always available.

At the other extreme, give a 1 to a poor listener, a very unfriendly person, or someone who is rarely available.

Give scores ranging from two to nine, of course, to adults who fall between the extremes.

	Good Listener	Friendly	Available
1. Mother or stepmother or foster mother	____	____	____
2. Father or stepfather or foster father	____	____	____
3. Adult sister or brother	____	____	____
4. Aunt or uncle	____	____	____
5. Grandmother or grandfather	____	____	____
6. Adult relative other than the above	____	____	____
7. A teacher	____	____	____
8. A counselor	____	____	____
9. A principal	____	____	____
10. A coach	____	____	____
11. A music director (or other director of special activities)	____	____	____
12. A minister, priest, or rabbi	____	____	____
13. A neighbor	____	____	____
14. An adult "boss" at your summer or after-school job	____	____	____
15. An admissions counselor at any college of interest to you	____	____	____
16. Other professional "helpers"	____	____	____
17. Any other adults (list by name):			
_____	____	____	____
_____	____	____	____
_____	____	____	____
_____	____	____	____
_____	____	____	____

structured to assist you in thinking systematically about the issue, rather than to establish a rating on a numerical scale.

As with Table I, circle 9s and 10s wherever they appear on your answer sheet. Any adult to whom you gave more than one 9 or 10 is worth considering seriously for the role of trusted adult.

You may or may not realize that there is at least one adult listed in Table II whom you probably do not yet know, but who is almost certain to score a 9 or 10 *in all three columns* once you have introduced yourself to her or him. That person is shown as number 15, "An admissions counselor at any college of interest to you."

Those adults—most of them are in their twenties—are hired by colleges and universities precisely because they are good listeners, friendly, and eager to help. And they are certainly available to you, since being available to high school juniors and seniors is what they are paid to do. Naturally each of them will be biased in favor of his or her own college, but most of them, especially as you get to know them better, will discuss frankly the advantages and disadvantages of their school as compared with others. Good admissions counselors will have your best interests at heart, just as any other trusted adult will.

If you have been thinking to this point that no adult could possibly be involved in your college choosing, I hope Table II has led you to think further about that. If it has not, please know that you certainly *can*, with careful attention to the ideas in the remaining chapters, make the ideal choice for yourself even without adult involvement. You will be missing an important ingredient in the choosing mixture, but you can still achieve the perfect fit if you are careful enough, thoughtful enough, and persistent enough.

"GROWN MEN DO CRY"

Bud Francis is a close friend of mine. I want to conclude this chapter with an article he wrote shortly after he took his third and youngest child—his and Carole's only daughter—to college.

The reason I want you to see this now, rather than in later chapters dealing with parents' roles or with the first year in college, is that you may have gotten the impression so far that fathers stand far removed from the college-choosing process. It is true that often it is the student's mother who gets deeply involved. But read Mr. Francis's words to see how the start of college looked through one father's eyes.

Bud Francis had urged his daughter, Laura, to stay in the region of their home. He drew a 500-mile radius around their home on a map and allowed her to pursue admission to any college that fell within it. Although Laura consulted regularly with both her parents about her progress, she had had a "favorite choice" since early in high school. The choice was hers and was obviously based upon her own strong personal preferences. It was almost exactly five-hundred miles away.

Here is her father's description:

...As president of a growing business, I have encountered change every day. Based on that conditioning process, it seems I would be immune to the side effects of change occurring in my personal life.

"Laura is special." These are the words her mother used to describe her from infancy.

When Laura was three months old, she had bronchitis and viral pneumonia. At the point of death, Laura was in an oxygen tent with the assorted tubes and other hospital paraphernalia when her mother appealed for divine help.

"Oh Lord, please let Laura live so that she can be a joy to others," her mom prayed. Laura recovered from her illness, and all through her childhood and into the teenage years she was certainly a joy to her parents and others around her. She always did her best in whatever pursuit she undertook.

In athletics she excelled in tennis and volleyball. In social life she was the president of her [high school] sorority and had a steady boyfriend. In her spiritual life, she was active in church work as well as ecumenical groups such as Young Life. That she was active is an understatement.

One project involved traveling with a group of young people to West Virginia to rebuild a house for an elderly coal miner with no family who was plagued with black lung. In academics she graduated from high school with honors.

Laura, now eighteen years old, was ready to go to the college she yearned for in her high school years, the University of North Carolina at Chapel Hill. Normally, the trip to North Carolina for orientation and enrollment would be one trip in which Mom and Dad would participate. A terminal illness of a close relative prohibited Mom from going, so Dad undertook the 500-mile-plus trip through the mountains to the Piedmont region of North Carolina with Laura. The trip would be no problem for Dad because he was an "old hand" at this process, having sent Laura's two older brothers to college.

During the drive, Laura was in a pensive mood, physically tired from many good-bye parties with friends over the past few days and the rigors of packing and preparing for college. She lounged comfortably in the car and spoke of recent events.

Occasionally a tear would appear in her eye as she realized she was facing a new chapter in her life. She would not be seeing old friends and relatives, and many new challenges awaited. Once when a tear appeared, she remarked to me, "Dad, I never see you cry." I replied, "It's all right to cry, Laura. I have cried two or three times in my life," though I could only remember one time in the last three decades.

We arrived at Chapel Hill and for the next two days attended parent and student orientation and indoctrination. We began the process of moving Laura into the large coed dormitory at the south side of the campus, which housed 900 students.

At the end of the second day, as we finished the unpacking process in Laura's room, it was already dark outside, and the dorm was still empty because only a few out-of-state freshmen had arrived. Laura and I were in her room moving luggage to storage, hanging pictures, and talking quietly. Her usual aplomb was returning as she efficiently arranged the room and made decisions concerning her new lifestyle.

We talked quietly, and Laura said, "You know, Dad, that I won't be coming home anymore."

"What do you mean, Laura?" I asked.

"This is my new home, Dad," she said.

"What about summers?"

"I will be visiting then only for a short time."

"What about after graduation?"

"I will be working on my own," she said.

Silence followed, and the impact of the hectic activities of the past few days began to hit me. This was our "little girl," who was not little anymore. A tear started to form in my eye, and I sensed the same in Laura. She looked at me and walked slowly over, sat in my lap, gave me a hug.

"Thank you so much for all your help," she said. We kissed each other and rose to proceed down the nine floors of the dorm to the lobby.

As I stepped out of the elevator I was brushing away the tears. When I saw others there in the lobby, she said, "Dad, don't worry. You said it was all right to cry."

We proceeded to the car because a new friend had invited her to come over to see her dorm room. As we drove to another section of the campus, she exclaimed, "You and Mom have always made things so secure for me, and now I feel insecure." She kissed me good-bye.

"Don't forget, Laura, call us on Sunday night with your new phone number." She promised she would.

"I love you, Daddy," she said as she stepped from the car into her new life.

"I love you, too, Laura."

My tears began to flow as I pulled away from the parking lot. I turned around and looked at her once more when I was on the street in front of the dorm. She had paused halfway up the sidewalk, head high, and was waving gently. "Good-bye, Daddy." I could not reply. This grown man was blinded by his own tears.   —V.W. "Bud" Francis III

CHAPTER ◇ 3

How Can I Be Certain?

Before we go another step, I want to acknowledge that the answer to the above question is always, "I cannot." Neither you nor I can be certain about decisions that involve the future. We choose to marry, to have children, to accept a job, to move to a new place, to buy a car, to buy a house—and yes, to go to college—without ever having absolute certainty that we have chosen well.

A degree of uncertainty exists in almost every decision, and learning to enjoy that aspect of life is a big part of learning to be a happy person. You can influence your own happiness, first by learning the characteristics of making good decisions, and second by learning to *work* to make your decision turn out well.

You may, for example, have decided at some point in your high school life to have an "exclusive relationship"— we used to call it "going steady." So you told your friend that you would date only her or him, you may have exchanged a ring or some other piece of jewelry as a symbol of the relationship, you told all your friends about it, and you two became a "couple" in everyone's eyes.

How certain were you that it was the right thing? How certain were you that it would work out well, that you both would be happy, and that it would go on indefinitely?

And how has it worked out? Have you both been happy? Will it continue indefinitely?

If it has worked well, if it looks as if it will continue for a long time, and if you two are like most of us, there are probably certain characteristics of how-you-did-it. One characteristic would be that you gave it some pretty careful thought at the start. You imagined how it would be, you talked to your closest friends about it, you spent a lot of time with your new person, and you did everything you could to test out the idea before making the commitment.

The second major characteristic of this relationship of yours, if it is like most that work well, is that you both worked at making it good. You did not merely set up expectations that the relationship would be perfect because you were both "in love." You hoped to be happy, but you decided that you would work to make yourself—and your partner—as happy as people can reasonably be.

Having decided to work at this, you did not slam the phone down when your partner said something irritating. You did not say, when he or she was in a bad mood and no fun to be with, "I never want to see you again." You worked to understand him or her, you talked through your problems, and you made the relationship workable by paying attention to it. Happiness does not just present itself to us. It usually is the result of thoughtful, concentrated effort.

What does this have to do with choosing a college? A great deal, in my opinion.

Those two major characteristics of deciding well apply as appropriately to the college choice as to the relationship choice. For the college decision, you must first put time and effort into the decision, finding out everything you realistically can about it. Having chosen, you relax with the fact that you researched the problem, consulted with a trusted adult, took into account your strong personal preferences, and made your choice thoughtfully. And then you work at making your choice succeed.

This chapter deals with the "thoughtful choosing" part of the process. In Chapter 1, I listed four action steps that I recommended taking immediately. The first was to assess yourself, which you did in Table I. The second was to involve either your parents or other adults you trust, and that was the subject of Chapter 2 and of Table II.

The third action step was: "Get *first-hand* information about any college you are seriously considering." The fourth was to maintain your objective of fitting yourself to a school in order to have the most supportive environment possible and thereby ensure your ultimate success: graduation.

This chapter, like all the others, assumes that you agree with the fourth step, and it therefore tries to show you how to do a good job with the third.

Next is this question: Just what is "first-hand information"? It is the sort of information you get from talking to students who attend a college in which you have some interest, from talking with a recent graduate of that college, from talking with an Admissions Counselor at the college, from talking to any other person who works there (the president, the professors, the custodians, the secretaries, the dining hall manager, and so on), and, above all, from spending some time *experiencing* what it is like to be there.

Everything else is second-hand, not first-hand. Some second-hand information does have importance. For example, you will certainly want a copy of the college's

Catalog. As mentioned earlier, you can have any college's Catalog for the asking.

The problem with second-hand information like the Catalog is that nearly every college in America has a nice looking Catalog that contains all of the "official" information you could possibly want. Reading the catalog is essential, in that it is the simplest way to find out how much it costs to go there, whether the college offers what you are interested in studying, whether it has a soccer or volleyball team you might want to try out for, and so on.

But the Catalog will not help you decide between one college and another unless you want to study something that only certain large institutions offer, such as aeronautical engineering. Almost every college, for example, offers an English major, a business major, a major in physical education, and the other most common areas of study.

To find the college that truly "fits" you so that you maximize your chances of being happy and of being successful (that is, graduating), you really have to go there and spend some time. And while you are there, you must do a better job than I did.

Maybe you cannot imagine going to a college and starting up conversations with people. Perhaps the following points will help:

1. The Admissions Counselors are hired because they know how to talk to prospective students. They are hired to be good at helping you find out everything you need to know. It is in their interest to convince you that you should come to their college.

2. When students enjoy their college, they are usually happy to sit down for a few minutes, or maybe for a few hours, and talk with you about what it is like to be a student there. The Admis-

sions Counselor will be glad to grab a student or two that she or he knows well, give the two or three of you a place to talk, and let you listen to their thoughts about the college experience. And do ask to talk to at least one freshman. That freshman will be better than anyone at giving you a feel for the college, because she or he will still be adjusting to the experience, will still be experimenting with how-to-do-things-right, and will still be thoughtful about the process. (At my school we have about thirty students, called the President's Association of Students, who actively assist with this process. Many other schools have similar organizations.)

3. The Admissions Counselors will also give you a tour of the buildings and grounds, so that you can see something of the campus.

4. The Admissions Counselors will arrange anything you want: lunch in the dining halls, an interview with a professor, an interview with a financial aid assistant who can help you figure out the costs, a talk with a coach, and even an hour visiting a class.

5. Beyond all these things that Admissions Counselors can arrange, you ought to spend some time by yourself, just walking around, and even starting up some conversations on your own.

All of that comprises a good example of what I mean by "first-hand experience" with a college. Believe me, after a day on campus you will have a much better sense of whether or not that college is the perfect fit for you than you can get from reading the Catalog and other materials.

But can you make yourself do all that? Let me advance two ideas in response to that question. The first has to do with your trusted adult or adults. The other has to do with something called "assertiveness."

In Chapter 2 I suggested that your trusted adult had possible roles well beyond merely reacting to your strong personal preferences. I suggested other possible roles: helping with notes to Admissions Offices, with letters, with phone calls, with obtaining and studying catalogs, with thinking about financial aid, and with planning a visit to a college campus (including transportation arrangements and details of interviews).

The point I want to make here is that regardless of whether you feel a little uncertain in handling this campus visit by yourself, you should enlist the help of the adult you decided upon. And if you did not decide on one or several potential helpful adults at that point, then go back to Table II and go through it again. It is important!

Consider this. I have a standing rule at my college that every high-school student who visits our campus is to be brought to my office for a visit, provided I am on campus. In all this time I can think of only two such students who arrived in my office (escorted by an Admissions Counselor, of course) without at least one other person with her or him. Usually the other person was a parent, a close friend, or a high school Guidance Counselor. Occasionally it was another relative, a neighbor, or some other adult who was trusted enough by the student to be asked to be part of the process.

As for the two who were not accompanied, one was a married woman with children, and the other was a young man who had completed a year at a military academy and was considering transferring to our school on a soccer scholarship. Those were special cases, certainly.

You have the fear, of course, that if an adult comes with you, "everybody" will think you are a child. "Everybody" will be thinking, "Look at her (him). Her parents have to bring her, just as if she were starting kindergarten." You also have the fear that your selected adult will embarrass you by asking questions you do not want asked, or by saying things about you—"Sally made all As in the ninth grade, but she flunked algebra in the tenth"—that will humiliate you.

If you have those thoughts, go back and review Chapter 2. One of my main points there was that you must select an adult based on the qualities listed in Table II. And I urged you to have that person read this book along with you.

So show your adult these paragraphs. Let her or him know that you fear being thought "a baby," and being embarrassed. Talk about the problem, and if you are dissatisfied with the response, select another adult. This is your life, and it is your decision. You do need assistance with certain aspects of the process, but you have the right to choose the kind of person who can help you in the way you want to be helped.

The other idea I want to advance in response to my question: "But can you make yourself do all that?" is the idea of "assertiveness." In any situation in which we feel called upon to make a response—gossip floating past our ears, a teacher misinterpreting a sentence in an essay, a visit to a college campus—we can do so in any of three ways. Our behavior can be labeled "aggressive," or "passive," or "assertive."

"Aggressive" behavior is marked by action to protect your own rights, but without regard for other people's rights. "Passive" behavior is the opposite: acknowledging other's rights, but not taking care of your own rights. "Assertive" behavior means doing both. You are assertive when you protect both your own and other people's rights.

Let me give a simple example. If, while in the cafeteria

line, you ask for the hamburger but the server mistakenly gives you the meat loaf, you have a choice of how to respond. An aggressive response would be marked by rudeness as you demand the hamburger, damaging the server's feelings in the process. A passive response would be marked by quiet acceptance of the mistake: You would just eat the meat loaf.

An assertive response would acknowledge the server's right to be treated with respect and courtesy. It would also acknowledge your right to choose the dish you prefer. You might say: "I'm sorry. I guess I didn't speak clearly enough. I wanted the hamburger, please." Of course, your tone of voice would be as important as your words, in this case and in most cases.

How would things turn out in this example? You would almost certainly get your hamburger. Would the server make the change graciously? Maybe. Maybe not.

Assertive behavior will never guarantee the response you want from the other person. It will probably get your own rights protected, and it has a far better chance than does aggressive behavior of getting the other person to respond as you hope. But we can never absolutely control others' behavior. Assertive behavior will usually be effective, but in interpersonal relationships there are no guarantees.

How does assertive behavior work in the process we are exploring? Try to think of the whole college choice process as something in which you have *rights*.

You have the right, for example, to study the prospective college "up close." You have the right to ask questions—detailed ones—about what it is like to go to school there. You have the right to go back to Table I and make a list of things you must find out about a college. You have the right to decide about the involvement of an adult in the process. You have the right to decide for yourself whom you want as your helper.

You have the right, once you get on campus, to ask to talk to a freshman, to eat a meal in the dining hall, to see a dormitory room, to visit a freshman English class, to talk with a professor, to talk with a coach, to get financial aid information, to observe or talk with someone in some special program in which you are interested, to ask for a copy of the Student Handbook, to talk to the campus minister or ministers, to see the campus radio station, the library, the athletic fields, the gymnasium, the science laboratories, the computer facilities for students, the chapel, the lounge, the bookstore, and so on and on. You, the prospective student, are deciding whether to invest four or five years of your life in this experience. You have the absolute *right* to receive all this information and more and to see all these things and more.

As for others' rights in this situation, you will want to consider those, too, in the process of being assertive. You will want to write or phone in advance to schedule your appointment with an Admissions Counselor, rather than showing up unannounced and demanding several hours of her or his time. You will want to give the Admissions Counselor an idea of the things you want to do so that she or he can work out your visit in the best way for everyone. Once on campus, you will want to be assertive with everyone with whom you speak, straightforwardly asking every question you need to ask, but with as much politeness, friendliness, and courtesy as you know how to show.

In advance of the visit, you will also have been assertive with your trusted adult, not only in selecting him or her, but in making clear just what role you want him or her to play—and not to play—during the visit. Assertiveness is a wonderful thing. And nobody "automatically" has it. Assertiveness is simply a way to behave. You can learn to behave that way mainly by practicing being that way.

It is much like learning to write as a first-grader, or to shoot a free throw in basketball, or to use a compass with confidence. A lot of uncertainty at first, followed gradually by an increase in skill, followed eventually by mastery and confidence. That is how assertiveness develops in anyone. Just start. Just keep doing it. The college decision is as good a place as any to begin to work on your assertiveness. Once developed, it will form a key to your success and happiness throughout life.

Before going on, let me suggest a list of items you should check on before and during your campus visit. Many of these items have already been mentioned in various places, but here they are laid out systematically for your consideration.

Items to Consider in Connection with a Campus Visit
1. Your own strong personal preferences (Table I).
2. Involvement of one or more trusted adults (Table II).
3. Reading of this book by your trusted adult so that she or he understands your process.
4. Preferably with your trusted adult, but if necessary without:
    a. calling or writing for a copy of the college catalog;
    b. discussing your interests and concerns by phone with an Admissions Counselor at the college of greatest interest to you;
    c. in that phone call or a later one, working out a schedule for your visit;
    d. the day before your visit phoning the Admis-

sions Counselor to confirm the details of your
schedule;

e. the day before and the day of your visit, checking and rechecking your list of items to do and
to learn;

f. checking your transportation plans to the college;

g. reviewing your "assertiveness" skills;

h. reviewing your "stress management" plans (see
Chapter 4).

5. On the day of the visit, preferably with your
trusted adult, but if necessary without:

a. arriving an hour early for your appointment so
that you can walk around the campus to get the
feel of the place;

b. appearing at the Admissions Office five minutes
early and assertively introducing yourself to the
receptionist;

c. making sure that during the course of your visit
you accomplish every one of the following that
has importance for you:

(1) talking with at least one freshman,

(2) conferring with a financial aid official,

(3) eating a meal in the dining hall,

(4) seeing a dormitory room,

(5) visiting a freshman English or math class,

(6) talking with a professor,

(7) talking with a coach,

(8) observing or talking with someone involved in a special program of interest to
you, such as the college newspaper, band,
or cheerleaders,

(9) talking with the campus minister,

(10) viewing the campus radio or television station,

(11) viewing some of the science laboratories,

(12) viewing the campus bookstore, the library, the athletic facilities, the computer facilities, the lounge, the chapel, and any other places of interest to you,

(13) obtaining copies of the Student Handbook, a course schedule for the next semester, and any other documents that the Admissions Counselor thinks might be useful to you,

(14) reviewing the catalog with your Admissions Counselor to make sure that, if you know what you want to study, the college offers those courses,

(15) touring the campus again, without the Admissions Counselor, and "assertively" asking questions of anyone you choose, especially questions that will tell you whether this college fits well with your strong personal preferences,

(16) while still on campus, reviewing Table I to make a thoughtful determination of whether this college's characteristics match your own strong personal preferences.

Like any list, this one will be helpful or not depending upon how carefully you use it. If you make the list a thoughtful part of your overall approach, it has the potential to guide you toward getting reliable first-hand information about any college you are seriously considering.

You will get better at the college-visit process as you go along. If you visit three colleges, you and your trusted adult will be better in the second visit than in the first and better in the third than in the second. Each time, be sure that you tailor the list to fit the situation. As you go along, you may change slightly in your goals. It is a good idea, in fact, to reexamine your responses to Table I before each college visit.

PATRICK WELSH

Mr. Welsh is a writer and an English teacher at T.C. Williams High School, Alexandria, Virginia. In the February 1989 issue of the magazine *Currents*, he issues some important warnings about the very people I am asking you to trust so much: the college Admissions Counselors.

Specifically, he refers to those Counselors from colleges that call themselves "selective," meaning that they admit only a few of the high school students who apply each year. Nearly all colleges are selective in that you must meet certain criteria, but colleges with the "selective" label may admit only one or two out of every ten students who apply. Although such colleges do not comprise the majority, they do account for large numbers of applications—and rejections—from high school students each year.

Here are some of Mr. Welsh's comments:

In the fall, the relationship between colleges and high school students is like a mating dance. "Colleges and universities begin wooing the high schools. Admissions people pour in acting as if they want our kids in the worst way," says Jim McClure, guidance director [at Mr. Welsh's school]. . . .

"They lead the kids on, making them believe they'll get accepted," he says. "Then in April, they start boasting to their alumni about all the applicants they rejected. I've never heard an admissions officer tell a kid not to apply, even though the kid may have no chance whatsoever of getting in."

Admissions officers aren't the only ones at fault for the stress high school students endure during the college selection process.... Successful parents tend to fixate on a small group of extremely competitive schools.... "Now more than ever, parents are interested in designer-label colleges," says Zola Schneider, an independent admissions counselor in Chevy Chase, Maryland....

So what can parents, admissions officers, and other adults do to lessen the ever-increasing tide of hysteria about where kids are going to college?

Parents might start by pointing out that there are many colleges kids haven't even heard of where they could not only be happy but also get a great education. Why not stress to students that their future success depends more on them than on the name of the college they attend?

The upper ranks of prestigious Washington law firms are filled with graduates of places such as Le Moyne, Loras, Iowa State, and Canisius. Lyndon Johnson, one of the most influential politicians of the century, went to Southwestern State Teachers College in San Marcos, Texas—not exactly a household name in higher education....

Kitty Porterfield, director of scholarships and financial aid at T.C. Williams [High School], thinks more college admissions officers should take the approach of Bill Hiss at Bates College. When Hiss comes to our school, he talks to students about how to find the college that's right for them rather than just selling

Bates. His approach helps not only the students but also the college. Bates' admissions officers save themselves time by not reviewing a flood of applications from kids who don't belong there. And, more important, Bates is less likely to get stuck with lots of discontented freshmen who will eventually transfer to another campus or spend four years grumbling.

Admissions officers should also be frank about tuition costs and their institutions' financial aid opportunities, Porterfield says. Each year she sees admissions officers lure top students into applying by promising, "We'll find a way to get you the money." Come April, these kids get in, but they don't get the financial aid. These types of bait-and-switch tactics leave students and parents with a bitter taste. . . .

By being honest with and sensitive to applicants and their families, colleges and universities will not only prevent unnecessary heartache. They'll also attract students who'll be the right match for their campuses.

Welsh and his colleagues at T.C. Williams, looking at your choice-of-college situation from their vantage point, see the same thing I see from mine. We see the importance of your matching yourself with a college that fits you and your needs, rather than feeling compelled to try to attend the most selective university in your region, or the one with the best football team, or the biggest, or the one your older brother attended.

And as Welsh has explained, not *all* Admissions Counselors will have your best interests at heart. You still must take the full responsibility for using Table I to make sure that you fit any college you seriously consider. If you do

that, and if you get the kind of first-hand information discussed in this chapter, you stand an excellent chance of
placing yourself in a college setting in which you may be
happier than you have ever been in your life.

How Do I Cope with the Stress?

Making the college decision is a stressful period in most people's lives. So is graduation from high school and the actual process of starting college. Here, at roughly the halfway point in this book, I want to take you on a detour.[1]

This detour examines the impact of stress on you and on your decisions. At its end we shall return to the main road of this book and consider the college choice in still more detail. But at that time you will be armed with such a thorough understanding of stress and its management that you will be better able to think about your choices and ultimately to live them.

Most of you have probably found reading this book to be stressful in itself. Realizing and coming to grips with the

---

[1] Several passages in this chapter are paraphrased or quoted from the author's earlier book, *Learning to Control Stress*, 1979, 1982, also published by Rosen Publishing Group.

fact that the college decision is one that you yourself will make, and that its effects will be with you throughout your life is enough to give anyone at least some anxiety. Working through Table I and Table II, thinking about selecting a trusted adult to assist you, preparing to telephone a college admissions office—few of us can cruise through such activities without feeling some pressure.

In January 1989 newspaper headlines announced: "Collegians Carry the Load of Pressure to Prosper," and "Freshmen Reporting More Stress: College Survey Finds Frequent Depression, Pressure to Succeed." The American Council on Education and the Higher Education Research Institute at the University of California at Los Angeles have conducted an annual survey since 1966 to measure trends among college students.

The most recent survey showed stress levels rising rapidly among college freshmen. The survey's authors suggested a possible link between their findings and the increased anxiety among high school students to get into the most selective colleges.

Whether or not that link exists, it is obvious to you by now that "getting into the most selective college," on the one hand, and "finding the perfect college fit," on the other, are often two completely different things. Furthermore, you will remember Dr. Jencks's study, which showed that the fundamental fact of "success in life" was not *which* college young people selected, but whether or not they actually *graduated* from college.

Keeping those two sentences firmly in mind can do as much for your stress levels as anything anyone can say to you. My most fundamental message is that you should be looking for your college "fit" so that your happiness will be as nearly assured as possible and your graduation will have the highest probability.

In *Learning to Control Stress*, I entitled one chapter, "How to Talk to Yourself," and referred to that chapter as the most important one in the book. I had explained earlier that stress is physical—it is something that happens in our bodies. Often we notice its results: headache, stomachache, "butterflies" in the stomach, perspiration, trembling voice, general nervousness, and so on.

But these results are caused by events that occur in our minds. To put it simply: We worry a lot.

All of us constantly talk to ourselves. What we say to ourselves determines, in part, what kind of people we become. In fact, the whole question of how stressed you are depends on what you *say* to yourself about what is happening (or what just happened or what may happen soon). You have noticed that some of your friends do not get upset about some kinds of things that can upset you considerably. Why is that? Probably because they are talking to themselves differently from the way you are.

You may think of air travel as something to worry about; one of your friends may think of it simply as exciting. A businessman or businesswoman who flies nearly every day may think of it as boring or annoying.

The way we think of a particular thing is the result of how we have learned to talk to ourselves about that thing. Not that we necessarily go into a long speech to ourselves every time something comes up. Sometimes we do, but more often we automatically think of it in a certain way— it's scary, or it's exciting, or it's relaxing. What we usually do not notice is that this "automatic" thinking is not really automatic at all. It just seems so because we have talked to ourselves in certain ways for most of our lives. And that means, fortunately, that we can change these "automatic" ways of thinking if we work on it.

Here is an example. In some of my classes I ask the

students to submit a short paper every week. The paper is an informal description of some stressful event that occurred in the student's life during the previous week, followed by an analysis of why the event was stressful and what he or she might have been able to do about it.

When the students first begin to write these papers each semester, they are full of sentences such as: "She makes me so mad when she . . ." or "Exams make me so anxious . . ." or "Parties and dances make me so nervous. . ." When I read such sentences, I cross out part of each one and change it to: "*I* make me so mad when I hear her say . . ." or "*I* make me so anxious when I take exams. . ." or "*I* make me so nervous when I go to parties and dances. . . ." As the semester goes on, the students get better and better at mentally *taking responsibility* for their own anger, anxiousness, nervousness, fear, depression, moodiness, and so on.

Nothing can make you mad except you. Nothing can make you anxious except you. Nothing can make you nervous except you. Nothing can make you afraid, depressed, or moody except you. You get mad if you talk to yourself in a certain way about what "she" said. You get anxious when you talk to yourself in a certain way about exams. You get nervous when you talk to yourself in a certain way about parties and dances. And so on, and on, and on. Your own self-talk generates the stress that you experience.

DR. ALBERT ELLIS

Dr. Ellis, noted psychologist and author, developed in the 1960's a twelve-item list of ideas associated with emotional disturbance. Over years of teaching and counseling, I have shortened and adapted Dr. Ellis's list so that it can apply to us "normal" people equally well.

Look carefully at each of these items. Ask yourself whether each one applies to you. Realize that each is a function of *how you choose to talk to yourself* about the events in your life:

1. Do you have the "automatic thought" that it is necessary for a person to be loved by everyone for everything she or he does? Or do your "automatic thoughts" focus more on *loving*?

2. Do you have the automatic thought that people having certain ideas or displaying certain actions are inherently terrible and should be punished or shunned? Or do your automatic thoughts focus more on these people's *behaviors* and on how they might be helped to change? Do you enjoy carrying grudges, or do you forgive easily?

3. When things go badly, do you have the automatic thought that you are facing a catastrophe? Or do your automatic thoughts suggest that you need to develop a plan to repair the damage?

4. Do you have the automatic thought that it is easier to avoid than to face life's difficulties and responsibilities? Or do your automatic thoughts acknowledge that postponing such issues usually makes things much worse?

5. Do you have the automatic thought that you must be completely competent and high achieving in all respects? Or do your automatic thoughts focus more on getting started and working steadily than on "being perfect"?

6. Do you have the automatic thought that once

something has strongly affected your life, it will always strongly affect it? Or do your automatic thoughts suggest that you can learn from past experiences but not be overly attached to or prejudiced by them?

7. Do you have the automatic thought that you must have certain and perfect control over everything? Or do your automatic thoughts acknowledge that life is full of chance and that it can be enjoyable and interesting despite (and partially because of) that fact?

What did you think?

If you are like most of us, you found yourself clearly described in at least several of these items' opening questions. Each opening question tends to be associated with high levels of stress; each follow-up question tends to be associated with lower levels of stress.

In particular, items 1, 3, 4, 5, and 7 apply to many high school students' college choice-point. Many students have automatic thoughts (self-talk) that lead them to be too concerned about what other people are going to think about them. Many view "bumps" in the process (such as difficulty in finding a satisfactory "trusted adult") as horrible setbacks rather than just something else to continue to work on. Many would rather postpone the whole thing. Many are perfectionists, even when perfection is a meaningless standard. And many want perfect control of inherently uncontrollable factors.

If none of these self-talk items applies to you, consider yourself fortunate indeed. If, like most of us, you see yourself in several of them, tackle them one at a time.

Any habit—*and automatic thoughts are nothing but habits*—can be changed by steady attention to it over a period of time. Usually a few weeks will modify even well-entrenched habits. So choose from the list the automatic thought that is of most concern to you. Use its number from the list as your cue.

If the item was the fifth one about being a perfectionist, use the number "5" as your cue. Write that "5" in your notebooks. Write "5" on little slips of paper and stick one in your wallet or purse, on your mirror, on your clock, or even tape one on your wrist.

When you see the number, mentally check yourself for signs of extreme perfectionism. You just made a 99 on math, instead of the 100 you expected. You see your mistake. Can you accept it? Can you forgive yourself? Can you *relax* with that 99?

Accepting a mistake or a fault does not, of course, mean that you should not attempt perfection, at least not when perfection is a realistic possibility. It merely means that when you do not reach perfection, you must learn to talk to yourself in ways that allow you to accept the error, and yourself, and to acknowledge that you are still a good, smart, able person who is capable of being both happy and successful. Just do it. This is important!

MORE SELF-TALK

There is one more aspect of self-talk that you should think about. It has to do with what I call the "rational questions." What automatic thought or thoughts do you have when you read each of the following words? Politicians. Ministers. Dentists. Principals. Coaches. Professional athletes. Supermarket checkout clerks. Garbage collectors.

How about this list of sentences? What automatic thought or thoughts do you have when you read each? Australians have a good sense of humor. Black widow spiders are common in Alabama. Journalism would be an exciting career.

Dr. David McElroy has done interesting research with such words and sentences. He and I are sure that from a stress management standpoint your automatic thoughts in response to such words or sentences have a great deal to do with your stress levels.

He and I would like your automatic response to come in the form of the three "rational questions," which are as follows:

1. Which one?
2. What do you mean?
3. How do you know?

Let's take a couple of examples.

What response did you have to the word "politicians"? Did you feel somewhat positive about the word and whatever ideas automatically came to mind? Or did you feel somewhat negative, perhaps having thoughts of campaign promises not kept or political scandals from the past?

From a stress management standpoint, the most appropriate automatic thought would be the first rational question: "Which one?" Having a response, that is, to what psychologists call an *abstraction* leads us rapidly into a fantasy world in which we continuously react to (and often become stressed by) ideas that do not necessarily connect to reality.

In other words, first get an answer to the question, "Which one?" and then experience your response. Are we talking about President Bush? Former President Roosevelt? Your current governor or mayor? Once you find the name of the real-life person or persons being referred to, it is safe to have your response, because now you are giving thought to real people with real policies that affect you and me.

How about another example? "Journalism would be an exciting career." What is the rational question to apply? The second, and then the third, of the rational questions: "What do you mean?" and "How do you know?"

You would be amazed at how many people embark upon some career because it "sounds exciting," without ever even speaking with or observing a person who is engaged in that career. Journalism? What kind? Working in what journalistic role? Working where? For whom? Many questions need answers before stating with certainty that a career would be exciting, but they are answerable.

Forming the *self-talk habit* of mentally asking, "Which one?" and "What do you mean?" and "How do you know?" is invaluable in managing stress levels. You need not ask the questions aloud. In fact, asking them at the wrong time and in the wrong tone of voice is often an invitation to an argument.

Mentally asking the rational questions will keep your anxiety and stress levels well in check, since they will keep you in touch with reality. True, reality itself can be stressful enough, but the fantasies we build take our stress levels far beyond the necessary limits.

My son, whom I discussed in Chapter 1 when I described his "false start" at one college, recently multiplied his stress levels to great heights, even though he knows the rational questions as well as I do.

Not long ago he came up for his annual job performance review. Failing to keep himself in touch with reality, he began to imagine that his boss would criticize him for innumerable mistakes or failures to take the right steps in various situations. He agonized for several weeks before this interview and eventually began to imagine that he would simply resign from his job in the face of such criticism.

Criticism? When the interview finally took place, my son found himself praised, complimented, and the recipient of a handsome pay raise.

How often do you generate anger, resentment, fear, anxiety, and all the other stress-related emotions because of imagined situations that turn out quite differently when they occur, if indeed they occur at all? If you are like most of us, the answer is, "More often than I like to recall."

Apply this self-talk self-treatment to your college choice. How are you talking to yourself about college? About the specifics that we have discussed in this book? Phoning an Admissions Counselor. Finding your trusted adult. Establishing your own strong personal preferences. Do not be anxious and stressed about fantasies! Just follow this book's guidelines and react to the realities that you encounter. Most young people find that the realities of the process are much more manageable than the fantasies they conjure up in their minds.

AN ILLUSTRATION

A number of years ago I wrote a book chapter in which I presented the following imaginary discussion in the halls of a high school. Notice how the rational questions take a potentially very stressful discussion toward something much less so. The topic is the upcoming award for Outstanding Senior.[2]

---

[2] Buckalew, M.W., "Using the Abstracting Process for Conflict Resolution," in *Classroom Exercises in General Semantics*, M. Morain (ed.), San Francisco: ISGS, 1980, pp. 101–106.

Student A: Shirley has just got to get that award; everybody admires her so much.

B: Yeah. She's sort of an ideal student in every way. The underclass students practically worship her.

C: Shirley's pregnant.

A: What!!! How do you know?

C: She's been all wrapped up with Steve in the halls and after the games, and you can see her starting to get fatter around the middle. Besides, all the senior boys are talking about it.

B: All the senior boys? Which ones?

C: Er...well, I guess I'm not sure exactly which ones. But I hear a lot of rumors.

A: Listen, C, that's the most vicious, tasteless, childish drivel I've ever heard in this school building.

C: You just want Shirley because her brother dates your sister!

D: Both of you are jerks! Bob Armstrong should have the award.

B: What do you mean?

D: He's the best pure student this school has had in years.

B: What do you mean by that?

D: Well, his grades and his intellectual leadership are so great.

B: But what does "intellectual leadership" mean?

D: You know—he started the Inquiry Club last year, and he's President of the National Honor Society, and he just got the scholarship to Center.

> B: Seems to me that somebody needs to specify what Outstanding Senior Award is supposed to mean. Then maybe it would be easy to figure out who should get it.

Right. So often we are stressed more because we do not ask the rational questions—we do not figure out what somebody else means, or even what we ourselves mean—than because there is really a conflict at hand.

Remember, too, that asking the rational questions aloud is a risk. Asking them in your own mind is excellent, easy, reliable *stress management*.

When you ask the questions aloud, the result may be to move the discussion to a realistic, manageable level. But the result may also be to start a fight, depending upon your tone of voice, the attitude of the other people, and a hundred other things. In stress management, dealing in your own mind with reality instead of fantasy is nearly always an anxiety-reducing, stress-reducing step to take. My strong suggestion is that, in addition to studying Dr. Ellis's list and working on any items that are problems for you, you also develop the habit of asking the three rational questions of yourself *before* you have stress responses to the situations you encounter daily.

Asking the rational questions of yourself continually in your college-choosing process makes very good sense. The risk in failing to do so is not merely that of operating at a higher stress level. It is also that of fitting yourself to a college that fits your fantasy view of yourself instead of the real you—the one who is actually going to go to college.

COUNTING DOWN

Counting Down is a modified version of one part of "Fantasy Relaxation Technique," a meditative procedure developed in the early 1970s by two of my colleagues at St. Lawrence University in Canton, New York. Theodore Renick and Hugh Gunnison[3] were very effective there in teaching their students to take several minutes regularly to implement Fantasy Relaxation.

Later I modified Fantasy Relaxation for use as an "action technique" for stress management. It had become apparent that most people, whether they were students or not, tended to have a hard time finding even the few minutes needed to do Fantasy Relaxation or any other meditative procedure. I took from Drs. Renick and Gunnison's technique the portion they called Counting Down, adapted it somewhat to make it usable as an action technique, and began to teach it to my students and to other audiences.

The great thing about Counting Down is that people will actually *do* it. It takes only a second or two, nobody else can tell that you are doing it, it becomes almost automatic after you have used it for a while, you can do it dozens or even hundreds of times a day, and it *works*. Counting Down is based upon the fact that when we are stressed, many things begin automatically to happen in our bodies: heart rate speeds up, blood pressure increases, hormones such as adrenaline begin to flow through the bloodstream, we begin to think less and less clearly (because of some of those hormones passing through the blood corridors in our brains), and so on.

Of all the literally hundreds of little and not-so-little events that start up in our bodies under stress, two of them—and only two of them—are easily controlled just by thinking: breathing rate and depth, and muscle tension.

[3] Gunnison, H. "Fantasy Relaxation Technique," *Personnel and Guidance Journal*, 55:299–300, 1976.

Think about it. Can you make your blood pressure go up or down just by thinking? How about your heart rate? Can you stop hormones from releasing just by saying so to yourself? Ah, but what about your breathing and your muscle tension? You can breathe deeply or shallowly; you can breathe quickly or slowly; you can tense a muscle or let it relax—all just by "giving commands" with your brain.

Fortunately, the individual pieces of your stress response connect to each other. If you control your breathing skillfully and relax your major muscle groups thoroughly, not very much will happen in the rest of your stress response.

Picture in your mind what happens when a basketball player is fouled. That player has been ripping up and down the court, running, faking, jumping, dribbling, playing defense, rebounding. Suddenly he or she is fouled. And everything stops.

The player walks to the foul line. The other nine players walk to their positions. The crowd stops screaming. Everyone stares at the player as he or she is handed the ball. Then what?

Usually, that player will, before shooting, take a deep breath, or maybe two. Then, before shooting, the player will shake out the muscles in the shooting hand and arm, or will at least bounce the ball repeatedly to help relax the muscles to be used in the shot. *That is stress management*.

Only then, after controlling muscle tension and controlling breathing rate and depth, will the player shoot the free throw. Players know that without relaxation few such shots will go in. Most players know that the greater the stress (such as in a tie game with one second left to play), the more important it is to get this kind of relaxation.

Why do players miss free throws? Why do some students find themselves unable to think clearly on tests? Why do some students find themselves petrified when standing in front of the class to give an oral book report? Usually, it is a case of poor stress management. Counting Down, an action technique that requires no "time out," is perfectly suited to help you perform well at the free-throw line, or to work your way through a history examination, or to walk to the front of the class to give your book report.

To see how to practice Counting Down and how to use it in public (which, as you will see, are two different things), refer to the accompanying box. Read the instructions carefully. Notice that you *practice* alone. But notice that when you publicly use Counting Down, it is done in a matter of seconds, with no one being aware that you are doing it.

Counting Down Procedure[4]

Counting Down is a procedure designed for use "in action." It requires no time out, and involves nothing which is visible to onlookers. Counting Down utilizes the psychophysiological principle of counterconditioning, and may be utilized dozens or even hundreds of times per day.

Counting Down practice is different from actual use of Counting Down in public. In the latter, one does nothing which is visible to other people. In practice, however, one purposely tenses muscles in a way that would be quite visible to onlookers.

Counting Down Practice:
1. Mentally divide your body into three parts—
   Part III: head, neck, shoulders, and arms.

---

[4] Buckalew, M.W., McDonagh, C.A., Brown, T., and Bruce, W.E., "An Academic Wellness Program: Stress Management Education," in *Health Promotion Education*, Opatz, J. (ed.). NWI: Stevens Point, Wisconsin, 1987, pp. 43–53.

Part II:　torso.

Part I:　legs.

2. Tense all muscles.
3. After eight-ten seconds, say to yourself the number "3", and relax all muscles in head, neck, shoulders, and arms.
4. After eight-ten seconds more, say to yourself the number "2," and relax all muscles in chest, abdomen, and back. **Concentrate** on making your breathing pattern and depth as normal as possible.
5. After eight-ten seconds more, say to yourself the number "1," and relax all leg muscles.
6. Concentrate now on how it feels to be completely relaxed, to have normal breathing, **and yet to be fully alert and ready to make hard decisions quickly, to ask appropriate questions without hesitation, and/or to think clearly about an exam question.**

Repeat the above procedure a half dozen times, moving faster through the Count Down each time, until the final one is executed as rapidly as one can say the three numbers.

Please note that in actual usage, the Count Down is done rapidly—that is, in three seconds or less. No purposeful tensing is done. The assumption behind the "action" use of this procedure is that as one becomes anxious, muscles are beginning to tense and respiration is beginning to increase in rate or depth, or both. This "psychophysiological cueing system," with regular use, will become second nature.

An example: in French class, a student is called upon to translate. She hears her name called, and during the several-second space between the instructor's calling of her name and the beginning of her translating, she Counts Down. That is, she quickly says to herself, "3,2,1." This is her cue, reminding her to relax muscles and to control respiration.

Having practiced this procedure slowly (as shown above), she is able quickly to recapture the relaxation necessary to think clearly under pressure. Having thus deflected her "alarm response," she begins to translate.

After looking carefully at the Counting Down instructions, imagine giving a book report to the class, using Counting Down as you do. Let's say that you are going to report on Mark Twain's *A Connecticut Yankee in King Arthur's Court*. You have read the book and found some of it funny, some of it boring, some of it interesting, and some of it confusing.

You have decided that in your report you will first describe briefly what takes place in the story and then discuss why you found it funny, boring, interesting, and confusing, mostly by giving examples from the book. Let's say you make some notes the night before and go to bed feeling sure that you have prepared satisfactorily, but not at all sure that you will be able to give the report without making a fool of yourself by forgetting what you wanted to say, by stammering and stuttering, by trembling uncontrollably, by blushing with embarrassment, by having your voice quake and squeak, and by perspiring visibly.

Now is the time to do the Counting Down *practice* session. Review the instructions. Imagine getting up in class the next day, walking to the front, looking at your classmates and your instructor, and delivering your report. Now do the Counting Down practice procedure. Repeat the procedure a half dozen times. Good. Now go to bed confident that you will do this well.

About twelve hours later you find yourself walking into English class, nervously worrying again about how you are going to look and sound in front of the class. After the bell has rung and your classmates have begun to settle down, you start to use Counting Down. Not the practice version, of course, but the public version.

Remember, Counting Down takes three seconds or less. You can Count Down repeatedly as you sit in class waiting for the instructor to call on you to give the report. Knowing how to do this puts you in control. You can actually control your stress response, and as you wait your turn you Count Down repeatedly to establish the slow heart rate and calm demeanor that you want to have when you speak.

Finally the teacher asks you to go to the front of the class and give your oral report on *The Connecticut Yankee*. When your name is called, you do not jump up instantly, blush all over, and stumble hurriedly and miserably to the front. Instead, you calmly take one more slow breath while you gather your notes together, you Count Down fairly slowly (in, say, three or four full seconds rather than one or two seconds) while you rise from your seat, and then, looking over your notes calmly, you make your way to the front of the room at a comfortable, leisurely pace.

When you arrive at the speaker's stand, you do not immediately begin to speak. You place your notes on the stand, Counting Down as you do so. Your eyes are still on the notes, and your breathing is slow. Your muscles are relaxed. Your Count Down has prepared you to deliver this report at a well-managed stress level.

You concentrate on your slow breathing, on your relaxed muscles, and on your opening sentence, *not* on the people in front of you. When you have completed at least one Count Down from your position in front of the class, and when your notes are arranged to your satisfaction, you begin to deliver your report slowly and carefully, looking up whenever you feel comfortable doing so. Between some of your sentences, do your Count Down.

Occasionally you may find yourself speeding up, beginning to stammer, or starting to say, "Uh...uh..." When that happens, close your mouth for a second, Count Down again, take your time, and feel the relaxation that the Count Down brings you. It is almost impossible to stammer or do any of the embarrassing things we all fear when we are thoroughly Counted Down, relaxed, and breathing normally.

Concentrate, too, on your notes. Focus on them and on your Count Down. Ignore the class, even when you occasionally glance up at them. They are hoping you do well, too. So is the teacher. Just go slow.

The end of the report will come surprisingly soon. When it does, do not clutch frantically at your notes and race to your seat. Repeat your earlier pattern of taking another Count Down, gathering your notes, and walking calmly to your seat, standing momentarily beside your desk rather than leaping into it.

Then seat yourself, take another slow Count Down while you put your notes away, and permit yourself to feel the glow of quiet satisfaction that we all feel after a job well done. You have been calm and poised, using your breathing control and relaxed muscles to stay in command of the situation. You deserve to feel good about yourself. Be proud. You were *good*.

Think now about how useful Counting Down will be in other stressful situations. Imagine phoning college Admissions Offices. Imagine driving to visit a college of interest to you. Imagine walking into an Admissions Office. Visualize a conversation with an Admissions Officer, or with a freshman at that college, or with a professor.

Realize that you have Counting Down with you all the time, ready to use whenever you recognize a stressful situation materializing. I have researched Counting Down for years. In one research project I attached students to biofeedback machines (which register stress levels through such instruments as muscle tension readers) when they came to my office to take "performance examinations" in my Stress Management course.[5] In this exam each student was asked to take ten minutes to reduce her or his stress levels, then five minutes to *increase* stress levels, and finally five more minutes to reduce stress levels again.

Results were fascinating. Ninety-seven percent of the students reduced stress levels in the first ten minutes; 72 percent increased stress levels in the next five minutes, and 93 percent reduced stress levels again in the final five minutes. These numbers would be impressive under any circumstances, but they are especially so in this case because 20 percent of each student's entire grade in the course was calculated from performance on this examination. They *had* to relax, and under great pressure.

How did they do it? Mostly by using Counting Down in conjunction with other techniques, such as repeating to themselves such "Self-Talk" items as 5 and 7 in the list earlier in this chapter. (Item 5: "Do you have the automatic thought that you must be completely competent and high achieving in all respects? Or do your automatic thoughts focus more on getting started and working steadily than on 'being perfect'?" Item 7: "Do you have the automatic thought that you must have certain and perfect control over everything? Or do your automatic thoughts acknowledge that life is full of chance, and that life can be enjoyable and interesting despite, and partially because of, this fact?")

YOUR MOTOR

Stress levels move up and down rapidly in most people. High stress can destroy performance. High stress can also

[5] Buckalew, M.W., and McDonagh, C. "Self-Regulation in an Undergraduate Psychology Course: Results from a Performance Examination," *Biofeedback and Self-Regulation*, Vol. 11, No. 4, 1986.

make you ill. Some of the hormones that your body produces under stress can reduce the effectiveness of your immune system, so that diseases you would normally defeat are able to "get" you.

Proper self-talk can improve both your performance and your health. Consistent use of action techniques like Counting Down can help both, as well. But you should also pay attention to what I call your "motor." That is your cardiovascular system. If this "CV system" works well, your body's ability to handle stress is greatly enhanced.

When I was a school principal, I drove to work every day in an old pickup truck. The school was at the top of a very steep hill. My truck always struggled with that hill, but not nearly so much after I had had the engined tuned. The difference was very noticeable. One day the truck would barely get to the top, coughing and wheezing all the way. The next day, after an engine tune-up, it would climb the hill without hesitating.

Hills are stressful for old trucks. Exams, sports and other contests, social events, and planning for college are stressful for high-school students. If your engine is running efficiently you can climb your hills much more easily than otherwise.

Your CV system will run efficiently if you exercise it and feed it a certain way. Exercise for stress management purposes does not need to be competitive or vigorous, but it must be regular. At least three times a week all of us should engage in some moderate activity that raises the heart rate to about 70 percent of maximum and keeps it at that level for twenty minutes or more.

Feeding the CV system is just as simple. Feed it less fat and more complex carbohydrate. When I was a high school and college athlete, we all thought that the thing to eat for the "pregame meal" was a huge steak. All that protein, we now know, did nothing for us at all. Luckily, that steak was always served with a baked potato. The complex carbohydrate from the potato gave our "motor" the fuel we required to perform in the contest at hand.

SUMMARY

Stress management is important. It is important equally for good performance and for good health. Thinking about college, doing something about it, starting off on the journey to higher education—these will be stressful times for most of you.

Practice good self-talk. Learn to Count Down. Exercise and eat better than you have in previous years. And then use this book to guide you through the process, so that you find yourself next year (or the year after) in a college or university in which you fit perfectly. Let me remind you once more of Dr. Christopher Jencks's study. Fundamental for success was not *which* college young people selected, but *graduation*! Learn to handle the stress of the process, and then get busy on the potentially enjoyable work of placing yourself "just right."

What Kind of College? Which One? What About My Friends?

I n Chapter 2 I referred to Brentwood High School and mentioned that this outstanding public school sends about nine of every ten graduates to college. I wrote that the college choice-point is so significant for most of its juniors and seniors that parents and counselors hold a panel discussion in midyear during which recent graduates discuss college choices and college life.

I promised then that I would return to that January 1989 panel discussion. Now is the time. In this chapter I want to let the Brentwood High panelists/graduates speak for themselves. In a later chapter you will hear more from these students, especially concerning their first year in college. Here is a list of the nine panelists:

- David Brooks—large state university
- Crista Carter—transferred from large state university to small private college
- Holly Carter—large private university
- Amy Depp—transferred from large state university to small private college
- Tom Eubank—large state university
- Darcy Fogelberg—large state university
- Alice Miles—large state university
- Carrie O'Neal—large state university
- Pat Patterson—large state university

Darcy: "Before I decided to go to _____, a large state university, I had been almost positive that I wanted to go to _____ (another large state university), which I had visited earlier. I think that the campus is very, very important. If you don't like a school's campus, you should think about that for a while. I mean, you're going to be there for years.

"But, before I made up my mind for sure, I visited the campus where I go to school now. I loved the campus, and that is almost the main thing that helped me decide to go to school there. I just think it's very important to do a visit."

Crista: "My mistake was going to _____ without ever having visited the campus. Once I got there, it was a culture shock for me. Eventually, after I called home almost every day, I began to like it better. But it was so hard at first.

"My first school—the one I never visited—was the largest campus in the nation, with 57,000 undergraduate students. I was used to being a big fish in a small pond. In high school, I did everything, I knew everybody, and I loved it.

"But when you go to a place that big, it's very difficult to find your place, to find your niche. I mean, I had a lot of friends, but it's really hard to become active, to become part of things. In some of my classes I had 700 students with me, and I could hardly see the board from my seat.

"I can remember Mom and Dad dropping me off. I had never been homesick in my life. I looked around and I said, 'You are not leaving me here!' But of course they left, and my claw marks were on the outside of the car. . . .

"At _____, where I transferred, I am much happier. There are only 1,800 students in the whole school. I love it. Now I don't like to come home quite so much.

"It's a lot easier to get financial aid and scholarship help at the smaller place, at least for people like me who are not All-America linebackers for the football team or something like that. It's true that at the big school there was a lot more to do in terms of the social life and the nightlife, but I just much prefer the small school because there's so much more individual attention."

David: "I didn't know where I wanted to go to college until April of my senior year at Brentwood, and then I decided to go to an orientation session up at _____. I got to meet some of the people there, got to look around the campus to get a sense for what it was all about. That's when I decided that this was where I wanted to go. Going to visit a place you're interested in will certainly help you make your decision, and will make deciding a lot easier, too.

"Just make sure that you like the campus, and that you

will be happy at the school you pick, *for your own reasons.* Don't go to a school just because your high school friends are going to go there, because you are going to make new friends in college, and you'll still have your closest high school friends anyway."

Crista: "At the small college [to which she transferred from the large university] there is more one-on-one. You get to know your professors. I know all my professors, and they all know me by name. You can go to them with problems you may have. I had several things come up last semester where I needed to have exams rescheduled just for me. They were glad to help me. There are only seventeen to twenty students in a class, so it's so much easier to learn. It's just amazing, the difference."

Darcy: "In my _____ class, the professor gives us a syllabus [an outline of the course and its requirements] at the start, and it says we have three tests, and one test might be a month from now. So, the professor goes on, and he lectures, and you take notes, and notes, and notes. . . . And that's all that is ever said, you know, until the day of the test. It's just your responsibility to keep up with that, and to know the day of the test, and to be ready for it.

"In high school, you can say, 'But you didn't tell us! You can't give us the test today; we're not ready!' You can't say that in college. You have to have read all the chapters and you have to have all the notes, and you have to be ready.

"One thing you have to realize if you're going to a big school is that your classes are going to be really big, and so you will have to do a lot of self-teaching. The teacher will give you some ideas, but it's not like in high school where the teacher says, 'A, B, C, and D are going to be on the test.' You will have to do a lot of self-teaching, and if you think you'll have trouble with that, a smaller school will probably give you a lot more special attention."

Tom: "You should know, though, that just because you're in a 200- or 300-person class, that's no excuse for not getting to know your teacher. That's no excuse just to sit in the back of the room and just show up every day. That teacher is usually more than happy to help you with any problems you may have, and the fact that they happen to have a big class doesn't mean that they aren't willing to help."

Amy: "I went to _____ my first year, and with 33,000 other students, you don't get to learn as much in the classes when there are maybe 500 people in the class with you. So, you have to study a lot on your own, at night. But at _____ where I go now, the classes are the same size as high school classes, with maybe twenty or thirty people, and you learn a lot more while you're in the classroom. Then there is not quite so much to do on your own, at night. It all depends on class size—and on what grade you want to make."

David: "In my school, we do have some small classes, even though the university is large. I've had some professors sit down with me to go over something I'm having trouble with, and they won't let me leave until they're satisfied that I understand it. There are some teachers that may blow you off, but that's just the luck of signing up for classes."

Pat: "Your teachers [at a large university] probably won't care if you go to class, and you don't usually get to know them, and they could care less if you're there. They'll never recognize whether you are there or not. They usually don't care if you are there, or if you pass or fail. When you get to be a junior or senior, you may get smaller classes with twenty or thirty students, and then the professors might know you some. Basically, though, it's always your choice about coming to class and about trying to get to know teachers."

Amy: "I loved _____ [the large state university from which she transferred]. I originally decided to transfer from there for personal reasons, to be at school with a particular guy. But at the last minute I decided not to go to that school either, so I stayed in this area and started to _____ [a small college]. I like the small school, too, though. Small school classes are easier to learn in, but the large school has a lot of opportunities that the smaller school doesn't."

Crista: "Be yourself. Don't try to be somebody you're not. And if you go somewhere and you're not happy, don't be scared to admit to yourself and to your parents that you made a wrong decision. Talk it over, and then just make a new decision."

You noticed that several of the themes of the Brentwood High School discussion are familiar. Those same themes have run throughout this book: the importance of visiting each college in which you have an interest, the importance of "fitting" yourself to a school, particularly in regard to its size, the importance of considering *your own* strong personal preferences as you make the decision, the certainty of finding new friends in your new setting, and the importance of being willing to acknowledge a mistake and to make a new decision any time you find yourself "stuck" in a situation that will not work out to your satisfaction.

In Table I you assessed your own needs. You rated your responses on a scale of 1 to 10 on such items as these:

- Grades are extremely important to me.
- It is important to me that all my teachers know my name.
- It is important to me that all my teachers enjoy teaching.
- I like to attend entertainment events (performances) frequently, such as concerts, movies, and other shows.
- I like to be able to attend large parties.
- It is important to me to have friends who think the way I do.

If you saved your answer sheet as I suggested, take a look at your answers now.

The table, you remember, was designed to give you a basis for knowing your own strong personal preferences. Are grades *extremely important* to you? If so, you may prefer a small college at which, as Amy noted, you will probably learn more in the classroom and, as almost all the panelists suggested, you stand a better chance of getting individual attention from your professors. Notice, too, though, that several of the panelists pointed out that if you are assertive enough you can get special attention even in large settings.

Is it extremely important to you that all your teachers know your name? That they enjoy teaching? If so, a small college may fit you better. In most small colleges professors view getting to know their students as a basic part of their responsibilities. But why, you may ask, is it more likely that small-college professors would enjoy teaching more than those at large universities? The answer to that requires a broad generalization: at small colleges professors are usually rewarded primarily for teaching excellence. At large universities professors are rewarded more for research and publication than for any other single facet of their performance. Consequently, people who love to teach tend to gravitate toward small institutions; people who love research try to place themselves in large universities. Can you love to do both? Sure. But most faculty members have a preference, and, being people like the rest of us, will tend to do best what they value the most.

How important to you are the outside-the-classroom aspects of college life? Here, large universities usually have great advantages over small colleges. Most large schools, in fact, publish a weekly events listing so filled with choices that a single student could not possibly do even half of them.

Equally important, however, to the issue of such activities is the question of the school's location. A small college in or near a large city may have few activities of its own, but that may not matter if movies, concerts, athletic contests, and other such events are within easy walking or driving distance. A small college in a small town that is an hour or more from a city is a different matter. You and your friends there will hear yourselves say often, "There's nothing to do here."

What you will mean, of course, is that there are fewer opportunities to *be entertained* than in cities or on large campuses. You will need to ask yourself, then, how important is it that I be entertained? And how does that balance with my interest in getting individual attention in the classroom? And how does all that balance with the primary goal in this whole college adventure: graduation! Let met remind you again: Successful people graduated from college; the question of which college made little difference.

Darcy talked about what she called "self-teaching." Will you be able to do that? Is "being entertained" a threat to your college success?

Some students who start college in a large city or on a large campus are so overwhelmed by the distractions that they fail academically because they lack the self-discipline and the willingness to self-teach. At a smaller college in a quieter setting they can succeed. Assess yourself on this point. How do you think you will be?

One final point of importance to some of you: Do you know already what academic field you want? Most high school students do not. Many who do find that they change, sometimes several times, once they arrive at college. But if you feel fairly certain about your academic field of interest, that, too, must be considered.

The academic field you need may not be offered at any school other than a large university. In fact, a few fields may be offered only at a very few such large universities nationwide. Get the school's catalog and check carefully.

Once you are sure that what you want is offered at the college in which, I hope, *your other strong personal preferences will be met*, take the next step. As discussed in Chapter 3, go to the campus and follow my suggestions about what to do while there. Make sure your visit includes a talk with one of the professors in the academic field you want. Your Admissions Counselor will arrange the meeting for you. This is essential because the catalog you have studied so carefully may be wrong.

Think about it. The catalog was written at least a year earlier, maybe more. Colleges and universities are continually changing. Plans may be in place that will strongly affect your academic choices, but they may not yet appear in your catalog. So go to the campus. Look around. Meet with at least one professor who teaches in your field. Tell him or her what you want, and then let this person talk for a while. You will go away knowing much more than you could possibly find out otherwise.

OTHER ISSUES OF IMPORTANCE

Is there still more to think about? Yes. And for some of you, these "other issues" may have a great deal of meaning.

For example, is it important to you that you have friends who think the way you do? Probably the best way to be sure of finding plenty of them is to attend a church-related school of your own faith (provided, of course, that you are a church member who takes your beliefs seriously). Not every student at a church-related school will be a member of that church, and some of the students there may be members who do not take their beliefs seriously, but most probably will.

How do you find out what colleges have a connection to your church? Ask your minister. He or she will be glad to supply you with a list of such schools.

The other way to be reasonably sure that you will have plenty of friends at college who view the world the way you do is to go to school close to home, especially if there is a small college near your home. You will find many students there who are from your area and have backgrounds similar to your own.

Some students, of course, have the opposite goal. One of their primary objectives is to attend a college in which there is diversity and in which they will encounter students from many backgrounds. If that is your goal, and if you

have the self-confidence to want to be challenged psychologically, emotionally, culturally, and religiously to that
extent, you will want to attend a large university that at-
tracts a national or even international student body and
probably is far from your home.

Be careful with such a choice. If you accept my premise
that the overriding college goal is to graduate successfully,
and, therefore, to place yourself in comfortable surround-
ings in which you will receive plenty of academic and other
attention, you must know that you are taking a risk. You
will certainly be "educated" outside the classroom in the
process of encountering innumerable students (and professors) with whom you have little or nothing in common,
but the chances of your feeling isolated, confused, and
unhappy are substantial. Failure of every kind may then
quickly ensue. That need not be fatal, of course. As Crista
told us, you just acknowledge your mistake and make a
new decision. Be careful with such a choice, just the same.
An error of this magnitude can be shattering to many
young people.

There are private colleges and there are public (or state-
supported) colleges. Which are best? Both. As always, the
answer depends on you. If your goal is to "fit" yourself as
perfectly as possible, the question of private or public may
make no difference at all.

The most consistent difference between the two is in the
cost of attendance. Tuition at a public school *in your state*
will almost always be lower than that at a public school out-
of-state or at any private school. Why? Because the tax-
payers of your state help support its public schools. If
you have a part-time job, part of what you earn probably
goes to support your state's schools through a tax on your
paycheck.

Even that can be misleading, though. Crista told us that

she qualified for a lot more financial aid at the small private college to which she transferred than at the huge public university at which she started.

The fact is that you will not have any idea how much it will cost to attend college until you apply, fill out the forms, and meet with someone from the Financial Aid Office. The process may take several months, so starting early is an excellent idea. Colleges or universities which, judging from the costs shown in the catalogs, you and your family could not possibly afford may turn out to be easily affordable when you receive your financial aid package.

Or maybe not. Maybe the school that you consider your best fit will not be easily affordable at all. Don't give up easily on your best fit. Think of this as an investment in your life. Your successful graduation will matter every day for the rest of your life. You can borrow money. You can work part time. You can take every other semester off and work full time. You can work for a year or two to save money before you begin. You can attend a less expensive school (which may not be the perfect fit) for a year or two, and then transfer. Usually, there is a way to handle financial problems connected with attending the college or university that fits you most perfectly.

And what about the differences among universities, colleges, community colleges, and vocational-technical colleges? In this book I have used the terms university and college interchangeably, since the difference really has to do only with size. Most universities are larger than most colleges, but there is a great deal of overlap. Some large colleges are many times the size of some small universities. Universities typically have more fields of study than colleges—for example, schools of architecture, or forestry, or nursing. As always, you cannot assume anything. Ask for the catalog. Talk to the people at the school. Then you will know.

A community college usually offers two-year programs, rather than the four-year programs offered by universities and colleges. With a two-year degree (usually called an associate degree), you can transfer to a four-year college or university (from which you then earn a bachelor's degree). Or you can stop there. Is a two-year degree as good as a four-year degree? Again, it depends on you. If you want a certain kind of job, the two-year degree may be just right. On the other hand, you will find yourself more limited in what you qualify for if you do not have the bachelor's degree.

Vocational-technical colleges are usually two-year institutions also. They generally prepare you very specifically to do a particular job, such as Emergency Medical Technician. If you know exactly what you want to do, and if a technical two-year degree will place you in that job, do not make the mistake of going to some other kind of school. On the other hand, as with any two-year degree, you will be more limited in what you can do later than if you have a four-year degree.

In Chapter 2, I wrote briefly of the liberal arts. I noted that almost all colleges and universities, and many community colleges as well, require you to complete something called (usually) the General Education Core of courses before you major in a particular academic area. These courses—English, history, mathematics, psychology, and other "broadening" subjects—are designed to turn you into an "educated man or woman."

Having completed this core of courses (which may take two of your four years in college), you are "liberally educated" in the eyes of the college and of the world and can then complete your major, which may be in a liberal arts area such as English or math but may be in something not considered liberal arts, such as business administration, or accounting, or physical education. No matter what your major, once you have completed your liberal arts core courses, your bachelor's degree will be a liberal arts bachelor's degree and will cause you to be viewed, rightly or wrongly, as an "educated person" in a way that no other academic achievement can. *This* is why Dr. Jencks found such a difference between "college graduates" and others when he studied adults' success in life. Those with liberal arts bachelor's degrees were viewed by the world as truly educated, and in a sense that others were not. It did not mean, of course, that a person could not succeed without a college degree or with a degree of some other kind. It meant that, in statistical terms, chances for "success" were distinctly better with that bachelor's degree than with any other kind of academic record.

GROUPS WITHIN GROUPS

Whether you choose large or small, you will be wise to consider becoming part of some smaller group, or maybe several of them, once you arrive at your college. I want to discuss this here, since it may have a bearing on what "kind" of college you select. It will come up again, though, in Chapter 6, "The First Year."

Even though the college I now lead is small, new groups continue to form every year. Just in the last few months, a number of the young women who live on campus decided to form a new sorority, and they have been successful in doing so. At about the same time, the black students decided to form a chapter of the Black Students of America. Both groups obtained faculty sponsors and then went through the process of becoming "official" on-campus organizations.

Why, on a small campus, would even smaller groups need to form? Students, being people, always need to feel that they "belong" to a group that values their membership. True, the group does not have to be official, and many small groups are built on informal friendships. But even such informal friendships are often best initiated and nurtured in the context of some club or organization that has already brought people together on the basis of some common interest or characteristic.

Do you remember Bill Vestal's letter in Chapter 1 and the wrenching experiences he endured when he and I were college classmates?

For Bill, the Methodist Student Center saved his life, in a way. It provided a home base for him without which he feels now he would have been completely lost.

All of us need something with which to identify. We can associate ourselves mentally with our college, but even the smallest college is too large to provide us with the comfort and emotional support we so often need, especially when we are trying to accomplish something difficult such as succeeding in college.

When I was in college, I became part of three smaller groups: a fraternity, an intercollegiate athletic team, and a church group. I belonged, technically, to several other "things." But those three groups formed my "identification units." I saw myself as a real part of each of them, and all my close friends eventually came from one or more of those groups.

In college, joining anything can be something of a risk, in that if you take it seriously your new organization will take some time away from studying. Be selective. This is another of those trade-offs in which you lose something and you gain somthing. If you are like most people, you will need to become part of some group smaller than the college itself. And if you are like most people, you will need to limit yourself to one, two, or maybe three of these to which you can commit without overextending yourself. You will receive the emotional nourishment you need without sacrificing so much study-time that your grades begin to suffer. Most students can find that kind of balance, provided they never lose sight of the ultimate goal: graduation from college.

CHANGE[1]

A strange genius came to America from Europe early in the 1900's and wrote a book called *Science and Sanity* (1933). In that book Alfred Korzybski suggested an unusual and useful way to think about change. He wrote that using this technique mentally might help us all behave "more sanely." In his opinion, most people behave most of the time in "unsane" ways—not "insane" but not quite "sane" either.

Korzybski called his technique "indexing and dating." He referred to the mental habit of qualifying the nouns and pronouns you read, those that you hear others speak, and those that you yourself speak or say to yourself.

Although this may sound mysterious at first, it is a fairly simple idea when applied to real life. When I was teaching at a university in the Rocky Mountain West, I had students each fall who were living away from home for the first time. They were mostly freshmen or transfer students. The

[1] This discussion of change is adapted from the author's earlier book, *Learning to Control Stress*, 1979, 1982, also published by Rosen Publishing Group.

transfer students had usually attended community colleges in their hometown for two years and, like the freshmen, were away from home for the first time.

One of the assignments that I gave this group was to write a paper about some stressful event from the previous week and then to analyze the event and his or her own reactions to it. Each fall I found that I could expect the students' papers just after Thanksgiving vacation to be unhappy. You would think otherwise, would you not? These students had been away from home for three months, had returned for the first time, and yet somehow had come back to college miserable.

Here is the way many of those late November papers began: "When I left home to come to college I was already looking forward to Thanksgiving vacation so that I could visit my parents, and my old high school, and my high school friends—and, of course, my boyfriend Robert who had dated me for junior and senior years in high school. But last week when the vacation came, I found that everything had completely changed. I could not even talk with my parents, I visited the high school and nobody paid any attention to me at all, my friends did not even seem like the same people I used to know so well, and even Bob seemed different. I just do not know what has happened."

So many of the papers sounded like that one that I began to return them just as written and ask the students to re-write the same paper for the following week. This time, however, they were to use indexing and dating through-out. The paper we just imagined would finally look like this:

"When I (August) left home (August) to come to college (August) I (August) was already looking forward to Thanks-giving vacation (November) so that I (November) could visit my parents (August!), and my old high school (June), and my high school friends (1968–1972)—and, of course, my boyfriend Robert (August) who had dated me (1970–72) for junior and senior years in high school. But last week when the vacation came, I (November) found that everything had completely changed. I (November) could not even talk with my parents (August), I (November) visited the high school (June) and nobody (Mrs. Jones, Coach Smith, Mr. Johnson) paid any attention to me at all, my friends (Sally, Gwen, Rosa) did not even seem like the same people (August) that I (August) used to know so well, and even Bob (August) seemed different. I (November) just do not know what has happened."

You cannot imagine what a difference that rewriting usually made. The students would come back to class with their papers, smiling and shaking their heads in the realization that they had been talking to themselves in ways that made no sense at all. They found that they (November) could not possibly talk to a *memory* (August or June or 1968–72).

This little exercise in indexing and dating had made them see that they themselves had changed in three months. We tend not to notice that we change because we live with ourselves all the time. When we are away from other people for several months, the changes that occur in them seem large to us, since we were not around them from day to day and could not experience their very gradual changing.

Rewriting the paper also helped my students to see that it was not true that "everything" was different or that "nobody" paid attention to them. In this case, it was Mrs. Jones, Coach Smith, and Mr. Johnson who were too busy with their classes to stop and get conspicuously excited at the sight of this recent graduate. The fact that several other teachers, coaches, and younger students were indeed excited to see her in the halls of her old high school escaped her notice because of the way she was talking to herself.

Think especially carefully about the pronoun "I." We use that word to describe ourselves throughout our entire lives. We say things like, "I did such and such when I was ten years old," or, "I am going to do such and such before I am thirty years old." But what is there about "I" (age ten) that is similar to "I" (age thirty)? It is exactly the same word. But is it exactly the same human being? Does it make good sense to think of yourself as the "same person" after twenty years of changing?

I, for example, am forty-eight years old as I write this. In 1950 I was ten years old. Was that "I"? Are any of my 1950 ideas, values, and hopes still "me" at age forty-eight? Do I look the same? Do I think the same? Do I want the same things?

The point is not that we should throw some of our words away. The point is that since we do not index and date in our minds as we think, talk, and listen or read, we often stress ourselves considerably by not realizing that we constantly change (and *should* constantly change), and that other people do also; that although we say "they" or "all of them" or "Central High School" or "nobody at all," what we really mean is "these certain, specific people at some certain, specific point in time." There is a considerable difference. Changing your talking/thinking habits so that you automatically "translate" what others say to you, as well as what you say to you, can have an important impact.

WHAT ABOUT MY FRIENDS?

In the Brentwood High School panel discussion, David said, "Just make sure that you like the campus, and that you will be happy at the school you pick, *for your own reasons*. Don't go to a school just because your high school friends are going to go there, because you are going to make new friends in college, and you'll still have your closest high school friends anyway."

Was David right?

I think he was exactly right.

About three weeks ago my phone rang. The voice on the other end said, "This is Tommy Smith. How are you doing?" Tommy and I had last talked when we were both in college (different colleges), roughly thirty years previously. Tommy had looked through his high school alumni directory, found that I lived a few hours' drive from him, and decided to call and see if we could get together some time. We have not done that yet, but we probably will.

How was the phone conversation with a friend I had not talked to in three decades? It was fun. Tommy had obviously changed. He talked about his investment business and discussed coaching Little League baseball, and he was clearly knowledgeable about both. When I knew him, I thought of him mainly as someone who could dribble well and shoot a good jump shot. Now, he is an adult! He knows things, thinks serious thoughts, and has "succeeded" with his life.

I still remember Paul Rollins, a high school friend with whom I rode to school every day for my junior and senior years, sitting in my room at home the summer before we all went off to college. We were talking about our friends, and where everybody was planning to start school, and how much fun it would be at Thanksgiving, at Christmas, and in the summers, when we would all be together again. Paul looked at me after a short silence and said, "But you know, don't you—it will *never* be the same."

Paul was right. It never has been the same. It never will be the same, either. The cold, hard fact is this: Most of your high school friendships will just stop.

You will not become enemies, of course, with all your friends. You will just go off on your own path, and they will go off on theirs. It *is* sad. In Chapter 1, I was trying to prepare you for that thought when I wrote that if you find a college in which you really do fit, you are likely to find more close friends than ever before, because you will be with people who made the same choice, probably for most of the same reasons. You will be living and studying with a lot of people who have similar interests and likes and dislikes. From such groups of people are close friendships formed.

From such groups, too, I must remind you, are wives and husbands found. You may fall in love in college, especially if you find the school that fits you best. Among all those other students of the opposite sex will be many who share your interests, your values, and your hopes and expectations. Imagine what that could mean, as you think about the question, "What about my friends?"

Marriage, one of the oldest social conventions known to humankind, will introduce a huge change in your friendship patterns. In the best marriages, the two people not only love each other, they become each other's best friends. Have you seen married couples like this? It is a beautiful thing to observe, and an even more wonderful thing to experience. He or she is *always* there for you. Your spouse is the person who knows you better than anyone ever has, and who will love you in good times and bad, no matter what. The two of you may have children and then may experience the pleasure of working together to raise them in ways that you think are right. Eventually, you will help them through the college choice-point in their lives, and you will be good at it, because you yourself learned to be good at it.

One more thought. In Chapter 4 I introduced you to Dr. Albert Ellis and gave you a list of "self-talk" items that I had derived over the years from his work.

I want to leave you in this chapter with the first of the seven items. When you ask yourself, "What about my friends?" and when you think about going to college and making new ones, you may be helped if you keep this question in mind: "Do you have the 'automatic thought' that it is necessary for a person to be loved by everyone for everything she or he does? Or do your 'automatic thoughts' focus more on *loving*?" Think about it.

CHAPTER 6

The First Year: How Will It Be?

We[1] want now to introduce you more thoroughly to the freshman experience in college. Our purpose is to let you see, mostly through the words of college students, what to expect when you arrive. It seems to us that the more you know about how it will be, the more confidence you are likely to have in the college-choosing process that you are about to begin.

The quotations from college students in this chapter fall in four categories: those from the panelists in the Brentwood High School panel discussion, those taken from three interviews with freshmen who were completing their first semester in college, excerpts from papers submitted in a psychology course required of freshmen at the university at

---

[1] Linda Hall and Walker Buckalew wrote this chapter together because Ms. Hall teaches a psychology course called "Personal Development," which is required of all entering students at the university at which she and Dr. Buckalew serve together.

which we teach, and quotations from college senior Karen Oldham.

As for the names of these students, we can give you only a few. The Brentwood High graduates were speaking "for the record," and have agreed to publication of their remarks. Also, Karen Oldham, Student Council President at our university, was quoted extensively in Chapter 1.

The three freshmen interviewed by Ms. Hall were speaking with the understanding that only their first names would appear in print. The numerous freshmen from whose papers we have taken excerpts were promised that they would not be identified at all.

All nine of the Brentwood High graduates are quoted in this chapter. You read their names and their college or university "types" at the start of Chapter 5. Here are their names again: David Brooks, Crista Carter, Holly Carter, Amy Depp, Tom Eubank, Darcy Fogelberg, Alice Miles, Carrie O'Neal, and Pat Patterson.

SOCIAL LIFE

Psychology student.   "The most difficult part of starting college this fall was deciding what my expectations for myself were. At first I thought that college would be classes in the morning and partying in the evening. After about three weeks of going out on Thursday nights (and sometimes a few days more) and regretting it the next day, I came to a realization that I didn't need that—that there was more to college than that.

"I had already been organized and I continued in that. I reassessed what I wanted, what I needed to do, and I realized that I had to be happy with myself and please myself rather than trying to do what pleased everyone else.

Since I've changed my way of viewing things, my life (classes, relaxation time, etc.) has gotten easier."

Tom. "You have to set certain limits as to what you will do and not do when you get into the real world, so to speak. A lot of people drink, and a lot of people drink a *lot*. A lot of people do drugs.

"I don't think you can judge someone or condemn someone for being in college and drinking. That's part of going to college, almost. It's a stage you go through. Almost your whole social life depends on that...."

Crista. "I'll have to disagree with Tom on that. To me, in high school there was more peer pressure to drink and to do things that you wouldn't feel comfortable doing than in college. It seems to me that in college people are more apt to accept you for who and what you are. If you don't drink, that's fine—you can still go out with the group.

"There are, sure, a lot of people who drink a lot. I was amazed at how much alcohol some people would consume. I just don't think your social life depends on it."

Alice. "That's true. The peer pressure does not get any worse. The peer pressure is certainly no worse at _____ than it was in high school. In college, you can go out, and nobody cares [what you do]. If you don't drink, they don't care. It doesn't make you any worse or better. But in high school it seems different. At least, it appears different."

Holly. "I think that in college you realize that you are the only one who is responsible for your actions. You're going to encounter alcohol and drugs anywhere you go. It's not like you're going to go home and see your parents, and they'll say, 'Oh, have you been drinking?'

"In college, nobody cares. It's just what you choose. And you just have to remember that you are responsible for whatever you do."

Darcy.   "I've seen less drug use in college than I saw in high school. Maybe it's there, and I just don't know...."

Crista.   "Someone asked me the other day, 'Are there a lot of drugs at school?' I said that I knew people who do drugs, and if I ever wanted them I'm sure that I could get them, but there's no pressure. The peer pressure is just not as great in college."

Tom.   "I've seen less drug use in college than at almost any time in my life. *Once you decide who you are and what you're going to do,* and you've said 'No' the first couple of times, people are not going to continue to ask you....

"Same thing with alcohol. If you make clear in the first couple of months that you don't want to be involved in serious drinking, you probably won't run with a drinking crowd."

Earl.   "The first time I came on campus was for Orientation and to take the placement tests. I came by myself. My mother wanted to come, but for some reason I didn't want her to. A lot of parents did come, so I guess she should have come, but she didn't.

"In Orientation the first day it was fun because I was writing my thoughts down. I noticed I was the only one who brought any kind of notebook, so I felt out of place....

"I noticed the room we were in, the Student Lounge; we never had anything like that in high school—a room just to group in. That was the first day I met Dan. We were taking the tests and he came in late. No one talked to each other.... But by the time we were finished with the test and had gone to lunch, everybody was already talking.

"We didn't know names yet, but we were talking about what we'd done that summer. It was like we were coming back from our junior and senior year and I just felt real close to everybody. I was excited, and on the way home I was excited about coming back and staying in the dorms."

Daniel. "Everybody should go to Orientation and really do it. If the school has something planned out, go do it because you'll meet a lot more people. I didn't, and that's why it was a lot harder for me. So do it, even if it seems kind of boring or nerdish—do it anyway.

"I also think it is really important to live on campus. I only know one person of all the ones that commute from home. I don't know any commuters that are real close friends with anybody on campus."

Psychology student. "The most difficult thing about college is living at home. My Mom just can't seem to understand I've changed a lot since last June. Things are getting better, but if I had it to do over, I'd live on campus."

Psychology student. "The most difficult part of college is the long drive from _____ to _____. I have also had problems making friends (since I don't live on campus). I have acquaintances, but not any really good friends that I can go do stuff with on the weekends."

Psychology student. "I feel that I fit in even though I do not live on campus.... Since day one people were friendly and did not care whether I was a freshman or what. Smiling faces were what I saw when I walked down the hall or around the campus anywhere.

"My newfound boyfriend is my biggest surprise because I did not expect to find one so soon."

Psychology student. "The most difficult thing that I've endured here is being away from my friends [back at home] most of the time. In the past I saw my [high school] friends every day, instead of once a week or so. It's not that I have a lot of good friends, but that they are very good friends and I miss them a lot.

"It seems that in the past I took them for granted, but when I'm around them now I usually have a lot more fun."

Psychology student. "The most difficult thing this semester for me has been the change from living at home to living in the dorm. I was not used to the responsibility as well as the freedom."

Psychology student. "The best part of college is being on my own. Also, meeting other people. I don't have many new friends, but the ones I do have are very good friends."

Psychology student. "The most difficult part of college for me has been adjusting to dorm life. I was not used to the noise and activity that is constantly present in the dorm. I was also not used to having no sleep.

"My roommate was a big adjustment for me. I have always had my own room, and sharing was very difficult for me at first. I was also accustomed to having my own phone and shower, and being close to my mother.

"The biggest surprise for me had to be how easy it was to meet people and make friends. Now I always have a friend to help me with homework or personal problems, which I've had plenty of. . . ."

Psychology student. "The most difficult thing about college has been trying to adjust to not knowing anyone and making new friends. At home I was very outgoing, because I had known everyone since I had been in pre-school. I had enjoyed meeting each new class that came to the high school.

"It's been hard not to know anyone. I have been studying a lot and am busy with activities during the day. . . .

"The best and most surprising things are that I am able to be on the tennis team and be a cheerleader. It helps me to stay busy so that I don't have to be by myself. . . ."

Earl. "I didn't get very much involved in my high school until my junior year, but I found out that I was easily accepted here in college. Coming here, I had been a big fish in a little pond, and was afraid of being the little fish in a big pond. But my college wasn't such a big pond. I was able to jump in right away."

Jean Marie. "I make friends pretty easily—my mouth, you know. I don't understand shy people, why they can't just walk up to someone and just say 'Hi.' I always do, if I see someone I don't know. It really wasn't hard for me at all to make friends here.

"Now my best friends are my college friends. My best friend from high school isn't my best friend any more. Well, she is—but she doesn't know anything about me now, and I don't know a lot about her.

"Freshman Orientation was the greatest thing ever. And the Orientation sessions helped so much, because I was really scared the first day of classes until I stepped in the building and saw all these people I already knew. I thought, 'Ah, this is cool! I can ask them for directions.' I like a small school and something with a good degree. Somewhere that makes you feel like you're needed. I would have a hard time in a big school.

"My advice to any freshman is: 'Don't lock yourself in your room. Go out. Don't be afraid to meet people, because they're just as scared as you are.'"

You heard from Karen Oldham in Chapter 1. Her words bear repeating here: "As far as friendships go in high school, . . . my time was so filled with clubs and other activities, and classes themselves took up so much of each day, that I didn't make a lot of close friendships. But when I came to college, this changed tremendously.

"Suddenly I had friends from all walks of life. I had rich friends, poor friends, extremely intelligent friends, not so intelligent friends, devoutly religious friends, and atheist friends. The diversity there was so much greater than it had been in high school.

"We have all matured a little bit. In high school kids are so immature that they can be cruel a lot of times. But all that changed from the very first day at college. . . . I've got the closest friends I have ever had in my life at college, and they have become a very important part of my life."

What summary comments about college "Social Life" can be made from these thoughts and ideas from college students?

1. You will probably find *less* peer pressure in college than you have found in high school.

2. Nevertheless, it is important to think through any questions about "who you are" before you arrive at college, and to make the decision to let your social life fit your real interests, needs, and values, rather than to try to adapt to your imagined idea of what everyone else wants you to be.

3. You will be responsible for your own actions and decisions in a way that you never have been before.

4. There is no consensus on the issue of whether it is better to live at home and commute to a nearby college, or to live on campus in the dormitories. This clearly depends on you, and the fact is that it probably does not matter unless you let it matter.

5. Friendships are there to be made, if you want to make them. Some initiative on your part helps! As Jean Marie just told us: "Don't lock yourself in your room. Go out. Don't be afraid to meet people, because they're just as scared as you are."

CLASSES AND PROFESSORS

In the previous chapter you read numerous comments by the Brentwood High panelists concerning college classes and professors. The discussion focused mostly on the differences in the size of the classes, the differences in the learning environments of large versus small schools, and the availability to individual students of the professors in large versus small schools. The consensus was that if you select a large university you should be prepared to do more of your learning on your own than in a small college in which more actual "teaching" occurs in the classrooms.

The Brentwood graduates agreed that the ability to do "self-teaching" was especially important in a large university, whereas in the smaller school the professors were more likely to become personally involved with you in their classes. Several of the panelists stressed, however, that being in large classes was no excuse for not getting to know your instructors. Some initiative by the students, they said, might be more needed in the large settings, but most professors would respond gladly to requests for assistance, no matter how large the classes or the university.

Here are more comments about the academic challenges of college from those and other students:

Psychology student. "The best thing is that I have done well, without going to pieces.... I finally feel like I've learned something. In high school, I did not. I've actually enjoyed going to all my classes, and I really liked all my instructors.

"I suppose the biggest surprise is how time-consuming college is. It's like a full-time job."

Psychology student. "The most difficult time that I had was getting organized for college life. It took a while for me to get used to managing my study time and my free time. Self-discipline was my biggest problem, because in high school I was forced to do my work or it reflected immediately on my grade. In college, work is not graded on a daily basis. Therefore, it is easier to say, 'I can do this later.'

"Keeping caught up and forcing myself to do the things I should do on time has made me realize that college life can be fun and I can have fun and free time while making good grades."

Psychology student. "The most difficult part of college is the organizing of my study time. I think every time I have a biology test I have a history test, too. When this happens I don't know what to study. Usually I am staying up late to study one or the other."

Psychology student. "One of the most difficult things is being self-motivated. Back home I was always told and reminded what I needed to do. At college we are more or less on our own. We are given an assignment and the only time we are reminded of it is right before we turn it in."

Psychology student. "The biggest surprise is my grades. I never dreamed that I would have a 3.0 GPA my first year.... My classes aren't easy, but I have adjusted to them all very well."

Psychology student. "The faculty to me seem not so friendly. They seem to be bothered by students' questions or requests for help."

Psychology student. "The most difficult part of this semester was probably being dedicated enough to go to class. I have not studied like I should have.... I guess you have to have a lot of willpower and desire to do well."

Psychology student. "The most difficult part of college life for me is having to be responsible. Having to wake myself up and say, 'You need to go to class,' is quite a change for me. It's difficult because I have to remember everything. There is no one there to remind me. I guess that's just how life gets."

Psychology student. "The most difficult thing about going to college was putting everything in perspective. When most of my friends were doing things I had to study. Sometimes I put 'fun' ahead of study. I had to get my priorities straight.

"The best thing is the realization that I can actually make it."

Psychology student. "The most difficult problem for me to overcome was just being on my own. Having to make the choice whether to go to class or to skip was a new experience.

"The surprise was the professors. They were totally different than what I expected. They were more concerned than I had ever imagined. They actually want the students to come to class. I thought they wouldn't care."

Daniel. "The academic part of college was a lot harder than high school, mainly because there was *no one there* to tell you that you had to get up and go to class.... Living away from home, the fact is that if you didn't want to get up and go to class you didn't have to. That surprised me.

"What really threw me more than anything is that you didn't go to class from 8:00 until 3:00 like in high school. You made your own schedule, and some days you might not even have a class at all.

"And then you have time to go back and take a nap before your next class. It was *hard to cope with* at first.

"As for classes themselves, they were a lot harder than in high school, but I had anticipated their being that hard. I spent a lot more time in the library, doing more research than in high school. There, you were given something to fill in the answers—working out of a textbook or workbook—but in college you're just given an assignment and you have to figure it out by yourself.

"Note-taking was a surprise, too. In high school I never

had to learn to do it well. Here at college, in some classes all you ever do is take notes. I had to learn how to take notes consistently.

"Another difficult aspect was that, where in high school you might have tests over each chapter, in college you might go weeks and weeks and then have a test over eight chapters and twelve pages of notes. It was hard because when the test finally came, there was so much material. . . . And sometimes it wasn't clear how the notes related to the chapters in the text. It was tough.

"I was sick for a while. The impact was not as bad as you might expect. Since we are in a small school, my sister would go see my professors and bring my assignments to me. It did hurt my grades, but probably not as badly as it would have, had I been in a large school."

Earl. "Classes were a slap in the face. Algebra! I hate math. I can't understand why I need it. If I'm going to teach English one day, why do I have to know what X equals? That class kept me up half the night—studying and worrying—and I was so sure that I was going to get an F that I didn't sell my book at the end of the semester, thinking I would be doing it all over again. I even told my Dad. Then I got a D and actually passed!

"In one of my major subjects [Education: preparing to become a teacher] I got a deficiency slip at midterm. That scared me. Last semester I did fine, and got a 2.5—about average. In high school I always got a little higher GPA, but it was easier to get by in high school.

"Going to classes on a two- or three-times weekly schedule is quite a change from the everyday schedule of high school. All the studying, following the syllabus, not being reminded of when things are due or when a test is coming, all the reading—it's all very different. I didn't discover the library until midsemester. That's when I woke up and realized that fun and games were over.

"It's true, too, that there is more deductive reasoning demanded of you. The professors want you to *think*. They aren't just handing you the knowledge."

Jean Marie: "I was really scared. All my teachers in high school had said that I was going to fail freshman English. That was just something they said happens to freshmen. I was really scared when I turned in my first theme. When I got a B I wanted to show it to my high school teacher!

"All my grades came along nicely. I was scared of Algebra because I've never liked it. I'm sure that if I developed a better attitude I'd be all right. Algebra is just always there. I ended up with a 3.4 for first semester.

"I had to study more. I had not had to study too much in high school. I find I study a lot more, and at different hours. I write themes better at 1:00 a.m., and I couldn't do that in high school because most of them were done in class, and I had to be in bed earlier. Now it's different. I developed new study hours.

"It was easy to skip classes and I did. . .well, in most of my classes there was a certain number that I could miss. If I was having a bad morning and just couldn't get up, I'd think, well, I've got that day and I just didn't go. That's good in some ways and bad in others."

We want to close this section with further comments from Karen Oldham, the only college senior involved in our interviews:

"I remember one class in particular, an Introduction to Philosophy class. In high school I was accustomed to just receiving information from the teacher, writing it down, and then writing it all back on a test. In this college class my freshman year, there was a lot of classroom interaction. The teacher had strong views about things that did not fit with mine, especially about religious faith.

"Never had I been so tested or challenged about my faith as I was in that class. And I felt like the teacher didn't like me. I felt like some of the class members didn't like me because of his reaction toward me, and I remember one time in particular that I got very upset during the class, and I felt like crying. But I held it in until the class was over and ran to the bathroom and just cried.

"I felt like I never wanted to go in that classroom again, and I couldn't wait until the end of the semester. While I was taking the class, I thought I hated it, but as it turned out in the end, I think it was probably one of the best classes I have ever had.

"During that semester in that Philosophy class, I learned more about myself, more about my beliefs, simply because I had been tested with them and had been presented with new ideas that challenged my own.

"That is a major aspect of the differences between high school and college. You will get things from professors that are challenging to your assumptions and beliefs. This is a function of becoming an educated person.

"To me, entering college for the first time was like entering first grade. When you are about five or six years old you walk into this huge building and you see all these new faces and you don't really know where you are supposed to go or what you are supposed to do.

"We fear the unknown. We leave the security of what we have grown accustomed to. We leave that for something new. But it is exciting and intriguing. And we must do it to become educated people."

*   *   *

Here is our summary of the collective wisdom of these
college students in regard to the issues grouped under the
heading of "classes and professors:"

1. Most of the students we interviewed were pleased
   that they had succeeded academically without
   "going to pieces."
2. Many actually enjoyed classes, but several found
   that real enjoyment came only *after* their decision
   to change their priorities to place *class attendance*
   and *studying* higher and "social life" lower. This
   was important especially because:
   a. grading will not be on a daily basis, so it will be
      easier to put things off;
   b. no one will force you to get out of bed and go to
      class;
   c. no one will keep track of your assignments,
      dates for exams, and dates papers and projects
      are due—unless you do;
   d. and, above all, unless your grades at the end of
      each semester are at a specified minimum level,
      you will not be allowed to register for the next
      semester. College will be over.

The context for all this is the basic premise that you have
encountered from the very beginning of this book, that
graduation from college is your key to a successful life. To
graduate from any college, you will have to set priorities
that *allow* you to succeed.

That will be the case even if you do as we urge you to
do—that is, find a college that fits you as perfectly as
possible. If the fit is good, graduation will be a much more
likely result than otherwise. But your priorities will still

have to place academics first and social life somewhere else on your list.

FEARS AND "HELP"

Crista: "At my school, we have an excellent Counseling Center. First, you are encouraged to go to see your R.A. [Residence Hall Advisor—a student, usually a junior or senior, designated to provide leadership to a dorm floor or part of a floor]. You go there first if you have a problem. Then, from there to the Counseling Center.

"I had a roommate last year who had a lot of difficult things going on—she went to the Counseling Center, and, you know, it's no big deal. Kids go there. It gives you somebody to talk to who knows how to be helpful."

Pat: "I'm a Resident Assistant at _____. It's amazing how many problems there are, and how many guys need to just sit down and talk about their problems for a while. 'Man, I've just got to talk about something,' they'll say.

"In my dorm there were about three or four suicide threats. The R.A.s are good, and dorm living is good, especially for freshmen. But R.A.s are by no means trained to counsel. They are trained to be listeners, and to listen to problems, and to direct people. . . . The Counselors really take good care of you."

Alice: "If there is a problem, or if you don't feel right about something, go and talk to your R.A. or to someone who is a professional. I thought that I was so ready to go to college. But it's scary. Don't think you're the only one out there that feels scared, or who's not quite right or something. There's a thousand other freshmen going through the same thing, so go and talk to somebody."

DORM LIFE

Tom: "If you don't know who you are going to room with, you can call the school, and they'll send you the names of people in your area who are going to go to your school. I went to _____ with a person I knew from high school, and that didn't last long.

"They'll put you in, then, with someone from a totally different area, and sometimes that doesn't work out either. I think it's always good to get someone from close to home."

Alice: "I roomed with a real good friend of mine from high school and grade school.... It is hard, though. My roommate is real honest with me. She says, 'Alice, pick up your mess.' You do get in arguments, and you do have to be honest, and you do have to learn to be considerate, and to think about them just as much as about yourself."

Earl: "I was really excited and wanting to meet my roommate. He didn't come to Orientation week, though. He finally came on Thursday before we had to register, and then he left the next Thursday because his girlfriend got pregnant. Then they gave me another roommate the next day. He scared me. He really did. Now I like him, though, and I think he'd do anything for you, but he wants you to do more for him.

"Anyway, he left, too. Decided he wasn't happy.

"Then they gave me someone else, but he wanted to room by himself.

"I was getting the idea that they just couldn't find anyone to room with me. Then finally I moved in with someone else. We're not that close. I can tell him things, but we're not that close. He's still a good guy and I like him.

"I had been excited about getting my roommate, and ended up with four different ones in the first semester. It was discouraging, but I feel like I'm the kind of guy who could get close to anyone."

Daniel: "I didn't have a roommate for a long time. I really wanted one. Then I got one, and didn't like him very much at first. But eventually I got to like him a lot."

Psychology student. "My biggest problem this year was my roommate. The smoke in my room from his pipe was terrible. Also, I found it very hard to get up and to be on time to classes when your roommate does not go to class. Roommates are important. Rooming with someone you already know is a good idea for freshmen."

Crista: "The worst part of college is sharing the bathroom. At home, my sister and I share the bathroom. In college, I have three suitemates, and so the four of us try to share. It is war! I mean, if you miss your shower time. . . ."

David: "In the dorm where I live, we have two bathrooms on my floor, and about fifty guys. It's amazing to me that some of these people never learned to flush the toilet. That, and waiting for shower time is hard. There's just not much privacy, so far as the bathroom is concerned."

Tom: "But you get to *know* those people! [Extended laughter from the audience. . . .]

"If you had your own private bathroom, there's a chance you'd never get to meet the guy three doors down the hall from you. But you see these people in the bathroom occasionally, and you find things to talk about. . . ."

Crista: "That's right. That is where you meet your friends. If you don't see them during the day, you find them in the bathroom at the end of the day, and then you finally talk. The bathrooms were kind of like the social gathering places for us."

PARENTS, CHURCH, EXERCISE

Tom: "Colleges have things called 'Parent Weekends.' Coming to see your kid at those times gives us a certain amount of time to prepare, and to clean our rooms and stuff like that. . . . A lot of parents come to campus for the games, especially in the fall, so that's a good time to get together, too."

Amy: "I enjoyed having my parents come to visit me. It's the only time you get to go out and try the restaurants and everything, and to get a good meal."

Crista: "When my parents came to visit me for the first time, I had two boys and four girls go out with us, because they were all so hungry."

David: "The church I've gone to here at home is the one I've attended all my life. It would be very hard for me to walk into a new church where I go to school, unless I could go with some friends. I haven't started, but I need to."

Tom: "Frankly, I was very surprised. I've always gone to church myself, but I didn't think many people would in college. But I got to school, and I found that all the girls went to church every Sunday. And they started wanting me to go with them. So I ended up going."

Pat: "Going to church is a good habit. Ask friends to go with you. There are a lot of guilty consciences at college— they'll say, 'Yeah, I better go after last night.'"

Darcy: "About exercise—most campuses have a recreation center or some kind of exercise center. There are always intramural sports, and people are always running or walking for exercise. There's plenty of opportunity to stay in shape."

Amy: "It's easy to find people to exercise with you in your dorm. Last year in my dorm the girls used to get together to do Jane Fonda exercise tapes. We'd have ten people crowded in the room and spilling over into the hallway, all doing Jane Fonda. You can find a lot of people to exercise with, and that makes it a lot easier.

"It's much harder now that I'm in an apartment by myself. I can't find people to exercise with. It's hard for me to exercise alone."

Tom: "I can tell you, you're going to put on weight in college. You don't eat balanced meals, and you eat a lot of junk food. I didn't do anything in high school to stay in shape, and I haven't done anything in college yet, but I'm going to have to because I can't fit into any of my pants. . . . It gets to a point where everybody says, 'Gee, have you put on weight?' Your parents may start to bug you about it. It would certainly behoove you to do something physical on a regular basis to stay in shape in college."

Our summary comments from this section follow:

"Help," Dorm Life, Parents, Church, Exercise

1. For help, talk to your roommate, go see your Residence Hall Advisor, or, if you need more than just a listener, do not hesitate for a minute to go to your school's Counseling Center (which may be the Dean of Students' Office, or may be a separate office). These people are there to help you and are very skilled at doing so.

2. Roommates are important. Our college students recommended rooming with someone from home, or at least from your home area, for your first semester. Roommate problems are distractions you do not want to have during your first months in college.

3. Parent visits can be very helpful. They should not be too frequent and should be planned jointly with the student.

4. If church has been important to you at home, it need have no less importance at college. Take the initiative to ask a friend to go with you.

5. "Being busy" does *not* count as exercise. It will be easy to put on weight and to become less healthy, unless you include regular exercise in your college schedule. Again, it will be your responsibility, not someone else's.

As we said earlier in this chapter, the context for these summary comments is the basic premise that you have encountered from the very beginning of this book: Graduation from college is your key to a successful life. To graduate from any college, you will have to set priorities that *allow* you to succeed.

Expect that to be true whether or not you find a college

that fits you as perfectly as possible. If the fit is good, graduation will be a much more likely result than otherwise. But your priorities will still have to be first and foremost on your academic performance and all that goes with it—class attendance, a daily study schedule, use of the library—and social life will have to be somewhere lower on your list than number one.

At the close of the Brentwood High School panel discussion, the moderator asked each panelist to give the audience a brief piece of advice. It seems appropriate to conclude this chapter with their responses:

Amy: "Go to class."

David: "Don't pick your school just because your friends from high school are going to go there. You'll make new friends in college, and you'll still have your high school friends anyway."

Carrie: "In the first year live in the dormitories—that's where you'll make most of your friends."

Alice: "Don't try to live all four years in the first semester."

Pat: "Don't be scared."

Darcy: "Get involved."

Tom: "Set goals. Make them high. But at the same time, set your limits."

Crista:　"Be yourself."

Holly:　"Realize that you're not the only one going into this. Your freshman classmates are going through the same things that you are. You are *not* alone."

CHAPTER ◇ 7

A Word to Parents

At the university in which we serve together, four orientation sessions are held each summer for incoming freshmen and transfer students. Each student selects one of the four and comes to campus for most of one day to take placement tests (so that he or she is assigned to just the right level of English and math); to receive first-hand information about the college, much of it from sophomores, juniors, and seniors who have volunteered to help; and to meet with an advisor who will work through the student's fall course schedule.

We urge parents to come, too. Almost all of them do. Except for lunch, we separate them from their children and present them with a different program of information.

We find—every time—that parents come to their child's orientation with many fears, most of them unnamed and undefined. In the process of spending a day talking with us, with other staff members and faculty, and, especially, with each other, they find that their fears can be named and can be defined.

Once named, defined, and concretized, fears become manageable for most people. The start of college is at least as difficult emotionally for most parents as it is for their children. It calls for a "letting go" and a willingness to acknowledge that the "child" has entered the "adult" world, never to return psychologically and emotionally.

Parents have given of themselves for nearly two decades to ensure each child's safe, secure, and certain advancement to this point: going off to college. When that point arrives, it can be an emotionally draining, wrenching experience.

At the close of Chapter 2 we included a published story, "Grown Men Do Cry," by V.W. Francis, in which he recounted his experience in taking his youngest child, and only daughter, to college. Here is a little of that dialogue again:

"We talked quietly, and Laura said, 'You know, Dad, that I won't be coming home any more.'

"'What do you mean, Laura?' I asked.

"'This is my new home, Dad,' she said.

"'What about summers?'

"'I will be visiting then only for a short time.'

"'What about after graduation?'

"'I will be working on my own,' she said.

"Silence followed and the impact of the hectic activities of the past few days began to hit me. This was our 'little girl,' who was not little any more. A tear started to form in my eye, and I sensed the same in Laura. . . .

"As I stepped out of the elevator, I was brushing away the tears. When I saw others there in the lobby, she said, 'Dad, don't worry. You said it was all right to cry. . . .'

"As we drove to another section of the campus, she exclaimed, 'You and Mom have always made things so secure for me, and now I feel insecure. . . .'

"'Don't forget, Laura, call us on Sunday night with your new phone number.' She promised she would."

What *should* parents do in the college choosing process? How *should* they feel? What role *do* they play?

Someone has said that the whole of parenting can be summed up by the impossible situation we face when we try to help our children learn to ride a bicycle for the first time. Too much support from us and they never get the "feel" of it. They do not learn to do it on their own. Too little support from us and they crash immediately. They may get hurt. They may give up.

There is no right or wrong way for parents to handle the college choosing process, but we do have these suggestions for your consideration. Ignore or modify them to fit your own family's needs. But do be aware that we have watched this process and participated in it from all three sides: We were college freshmen ourselves once, we are parents of grown children who have been college freshmen, and we have worked in college settings for a long time.

- Being emotional about the event is appropriate. This *is* the day your child leaves you in a very obvious, very permanent way. Your child is not your child from this point forward—not in the sense that she or he has been until now. And you are not her or his parent from this point forward—not in the previous sense. This marks the start of a new relationship with this young person whom you have raised from infancy. Parents who figure that out, and act accordingly, will probably hear from their grown children remarkably often.
- Chapter 2 was entitled "Who Decides?" In it, the high school junior or senior was urged to involve a

"trusted adult" in the process. Can you be a "trusted adult" for your own children? Can you work with your soon-to-be college freshman, talking with her or him about Table I in which the student lists "strong personal preferences" for college? Can you respect those preferences and then assist your child, if she or he requests, in the process of matching those preferences to a college that fits them? We hope so. But if you cannot, we hope you will do the next best thing, and that is to encourage your child to connect with a "trusted adult" other than your-self—a teacher, counselor, relative, neighbor—any adult who can serve as a good sounding board for your daughter or son.

• One of the most effective ways in which you can be supportive, yet not interfering, is to concentrate on setting a climate in your household that says to your child that you know college is important, that you are prepared for and hoping for your child's enroll-ment in college, and that you are ready to assist with any details, if asked. If you create that climate suc-cessfully, your child may ask you to read this whole book, for example. If so, we hope you will. That may give you a clearer sense of how all of this looks to her or him than most other approaches.

• Bear in mind our most basic point. It is your child's *graduation* from college that ultimately will matter in her or his adult lifetime. Do not confuse a col-lege's "status" with its "goodness of fit" for your child. The two may not be the same.

Adults' memories of their own childhood are often grossly distorted. Many adults recall grade school as a time when they just played and when responsibilities were few.

We have found, in contrast, that youngsters of elementary school age are usually just as highly stressed as anyone in the entire American population. Have you ever talked—really talked—with a child who has left her or his lunch money at home? It is no small matter. Not to that child.

Similarly, many adults' memories of their high school life, of their own college choice, and of their college life are filled with "selective forgetting." These times are recalled as low-pressure or even no-pressure periods when life was good and fun. Consider this quotation from a recent issue of *Money* magazine (May 1989), much of which dealt with the college-choosing process. A young high school senior from a Cleveland suburb is talking: "'You get pressure from everybody—the school, parents, friends.... I know it sounds irrational, but I'm worried that if I pick the wrong place [to go to college] I won't have any friends and won't get a job.' Still, _____ tries to be philosophical. 'I really think that my parents had such a good time at college that through me they are looking forward to going back,' she says. The tough part, she adds, 'They want to go to _____.'"

As you might guess, "they," this young student's parents, want to go to an extremely prestigious university. Does it truly fit their daughter's needs? Have they even asked themselves—or her—that question?

For your child's sake, ask it. By listening very carefully to the answer, you may then allow yourself to give your child one of the most valuable of the many gifts you have bestowed in her or his lifetime.

Index